CLEP® Introduction to Sociology

Gotham City Ventures, LLC

500 Westover Dr. #6479

Sanford, NC 27330

http://www.gothamcityventures.com/

ISBN: 978-0-9964591-4-3

Printed in the USA

Disclaimer/Liability Release:

Steps to Achieving Success!

Step 1- Test Taking/Study Skills Review

Gain knowledge in test taking and study skills with over 25 pages of review! Increase your chances of passing the exam by determining your learning style, how to study well and strategies for approaching exam questions.

Step 2- Complete Content Review

Focus on the exam content with a comprehensive review. CreditPREP provides you with a well written and organized presentation of content within this manual and access to online, mobile friendly flashcards. These flashcards allow you to take advantage of every spare moment in your hectic life! Please utilize this valuable resource with the instructions below:

FLASHCARD ACCESS:

Please go to www.gothamcitypublishing.com

Click on CreditPREP Flashcards Registration

Follow the Directions Provided to Access the Flashcards

Step 3- Test Your Knowledge

Use the full length practice exam provided at the end of this manual to determine your knowledge of Sociology. Use the results of this exam to efficiently focus your final studying efforts.

Step 4- Take Your Exam

Apply the credits earned toward your college degree and future career!!

Table of Contents

Preparing for your Exam

Chances are if you are reading this, you are a student looking to perform well on an upcoming test. Congratulations, you have taken the first step in achieving that goal. Yes, you have purchased this text, but more importantly this means you have determined to seek success and do what it takes to achieve this success. This means you are already in the right mindset to begin…so why don't we do just that and get started?

Taking a test and performing well is much like a sport. Consider the test to be the "big game" that students face over and over. Every athlete knows the importance of preparing for the game through practice, drills, and training. Just preparing is not enough; the athlete also knows the rules for his or her chosen sport and has developed the ability to remain calm under pressure. Each of these three skills comes together to allow the athlete to perform to the best of their ability and hopefully win the "big game". As a student, you have no doubt heard more than once that tests are designed to demonstrate your knowledge of the subject matter, and while that is true, this is not the entire picture. We have all encountered that student who studies less than everyone yet manages to pass or even get an "A" on the tests they take. Chances are this student not only knows the subject matter, but they know how to play the game. This text is designed to help you understand those "rules" and develop skills that will make you a master test taker. This guide will in no way substitute for knowledge of subject matter, but will certainly assist you in making sure that your test accurately demonstrates that knowledge and that the "rules of the game" operate in your favor. As we move forward, we are going to analyze some study skills that will help you acquire the subject matter knowledge necessary for your test, learn a few test-taking skills that will help you "play the game" even better, and examine how to work well under pressure (relive some of the test anxiety).

Study Skills

Ask almost anyone and they will tell you that the key to success on a test is to know the subject materials for which you are being tested. As we already mentioned, this is only part of the puzzle, but it is an important part. Thus, it is where we will begin our journey together – how to best acquire this subject matter expertise. Our goal here is to help you make the most of the time you invest for studying so that you gain the most knowledge possible in the time you commit to studying.

One of the most important things you can do, as a student, is to determine your learning style. This knowledge will serve you not only for this test, but for every class you ever take. There are a myriad of online quizzes that will help you identify your learning style, but for the sake of brevity we are going to discuss the five basic learning styles here. Chances are you already know how you learn best, even if you have never formally addressed this topic. The five learning styles are described below.

1. Visual learning – has a preference for learning through pictures, graphs, and spatial understanding.

2. Auditory – sometimes called musical – learns best through sound and lectures.
3. Verbal – sometimes called linguistic – process information through words both verbal and written.
4. Kinesthetic – this learner processes by feeling, sensing, and doing
5. Logical – sometimes called mathematical – uses logic and reasoning

If you are a **visual** learner you will want to spend time making graphs, charts, timelines, maps, and pictures that will help you understand the materials. You are going to remember far more about a picture, than information you simply read. If you are an **auditory** learner, then you are one in a small percentage of students who actually do learn through the lecture model that most of western education is built upon. The auditory learner will do best by reading texts books aloud so that they are not simply reading, but hearing the text. Much like the auditory learner, the **verbal** learner should also read test materials aloud. In this case, it is not hearing the content, but in verbalizing it. In addition to spoken word, the verbal learner also learns well by writing information. This makes the practice of note-taking especially beneficial to this learner. The **kinesthetic** learner is often the most challenging for teachers and professors to address. It is the kinesthetic learner who learns best by actually "doing". If you are this type of learner then you need to feel, hold, and manipulate objects in order to best understand the content. This type of learner will learn better while moving around and seldom studies well at a typical desk. Finally, the **logical** learner needs to understand the "why" behind ideas and concepts. The logical learner needs to see connections and reasons behind the information. Memorization of facts does not typically serve the logical learner as well as a thorough understanding of how the concepts relate to one another. It is important to note here that while one primary sense is usually tied to your learning style, you should incorporate as many senses as possible into your learning routine. So for the visual learner, it is imperative that they see the information in displayed form, but they will also enhance their memory be utilizing their auditory, verbal, and kinesthetic skills. Remember the more senses you can involve in the learning process the better. Don't be afraid to draw, read aloud, sing, or create objects that can be moved in order to see the logic and connections behind the facts.

In addition to the five different learning styles, there are two additional styles that some authors have added. These two are the solitary and social learner. These two types of learners can be found in conjunction with any of the above five learning styles. For example, one could be a solitary visual learner. As the name implies, the solitary learner prefers to learn alone while the social learner prefers learning in the group setting. While the solitary learner is likely to be found alone in the library, the social learner gravitates toward study groups and enjoys group projects that the solitary learner often dreads.

There has been much debate over the years regarding the best time of day to study. The short answer is, there is no one correct answer. The best time of day for study is completely student dependent. If an individual is more alert in the morning then they should study in the morning. If the student is better in the evening, then study in the evening. Most fathers are fond of reminding their children that "you can't hoot with the owls and soar with the eagles." Of course, the preference is typically that you soar with the morning eagles and avoid the night owls as much as possible. However, the main idea serves as a great reminder for students – if you are a morning person make sure to get enough rest to rise early and make use of that time. If you are indeed a night owl, then sleep in and be sure you devote the evening time to study, not just socializing with friends.

With the preliminaries out of the way, let us dive into some more hands on considerations that will help you make the most of your study time.

1. Prepare your space –
   a. Do not study in your bed. Our bodies are conditioned to see the bed as a place of rest and relaxation. By attempting to study in bed, we are constantly fighting the ingrained habit of our bodies. In addition, it can be difficult to fight the constant temptation to take a "quick cat nap" that turns into an hour or two of lost time.
   b. If you do not study in bed, where should you study? Really just about anywhere else that works for you and fits your learning style. Consider a dedicated space that you use only for study. The more you use the space the more your brain will begin to equate the space with productive study.
   c. For most students, a desk really is the best option as it not only sets the tone for study and work but also promotes good posture. Many kinesthetic learners benefit from a standing desk or a chair that allows for movement.
   d. Consider the lighting. Select a space that has good natural light and allows for good artificial light to be added if studying at night. In seeking natural light be cautious of windows. While they do provide great natural light, they can also be a source of distraction. If possible consider this in the placement of your desk. Desks placed to the side of a window allow for good light, but the temptation to gaze into the outdoors is limited by not being situated directly in front of you.
   e. Gather all your materials. Make sure you study space is adequately stocked with all the necessary materials: books, pens and pencils, paper, computer, printer, etc.
   f. Select appropriate music. For most learning styles, music that is instrumental is best for learning. This prevents one from using part of the brain to sing along instead of being focused on the topic at hand. For the auditory or musical learner, music can be especially powerful as subject material can be tied to the music for better understanding and recall.

2. Create a schedule for study. Determine what topics will be covered by your test and how many days you have to study for the exam. Plan out what topics you will study each day in order to be prepared for the test. Do not plan on studying any new material the night before the exam, as cramming is never a good option. Be sure to devote more time to topics that are unfamiliar or difficult.

3. Use a timer. Set your timer for 20 or 25 minutes. Studies show that the optimal time to study is in 20 to 25 minute segments with a 5 to 10 minute break between each. Your brain is actually best at remembering the first and last thing that you study. Therefore these short segments give you more first and last items. These short segments are short enough to maintain attention (even for those with ADD or ADHD) and long enough to study a substantial amount of information. During your break get up and move

around. Be sure your whole body is involved. The physical activity keeps your blood flowing and gives your brain a chance to take a break, without shutting down completely.

4. Study in "chunks". As we mentioned earlier your brain is great at remembering the first and last items on which you focus attention. Use this fact to your advantage by breaking information into lists or chunks of 3 to 5 items. This allows for more first and lasts in the set of information and uses your brains built in systems to your advantage.

5. Concentrate. It seems like the simplest advice, but the importance of concentration cannot be overstated. Concentration is the self-discipline of studying. Studying is not a passive skill (as much as all students wish it was). Studying is an active sport. You must engage your brain. If you struggle with concentration or suffer from ADD/ADHD consider removing anything that might distract you. For this author this meant going to the top floor of the library where the "quite rule" was strictly enforced, finding an enclosed study area where there were no visual distractions, and putting earplugs in so that not even the turning of pages could distract me. It soon became apparent that an hour spent in this environment was far more productive than 2 or 3 hours trying to study in a dorm room or even a more social area of the library. Do not be afraid to do what it takes to make concentration easier, it is a difficult discipline to build.

6. DO NOT use a highlighter when studying. A highlighter may be beneficial in marking items to be studied at a later time, but that is precisely what makes it such a poor tool for studying. The best use for a highlighter is in a fast paced lecture when something needs to be noted for later study. However, when studying as an individual the highlighter often serves as a mark of procrastination. Instead of highlighting the text to come back to later, take the time to devote it to memory. If the information is too in-depth or is a bit off topic, make a note on a separate piece of paper to come back and study further. The simple act of writing it down instead of highlighting begins the learning process. Make every attempt to understand and process information before moving along to another topic and instead of highlighting for later study.

7. Create connections. The more you can connect a new concept to something you already know the better your learning and recall will be. For visual learners, these connections should be drawn in pictures, flow charts or graphs. For the kinesthetic learner, as much as possible, the connections should be acted out or put into motions.

8. Use all of your senses. As much as possible try to engage all of your senses when studying. It is understood that your sight is always part of studying. Include your speech (which we know is not a true sense) and hearing in your study. Instead of just reading material silently "in your head", read it out loud. This engages three aspects of your brain: sight, hearing, and speech which make it more likely you will remember the content. If there is a way you can integrate the whole body into the concept then do so.

9. Study items from broad concepts to minor details. As you begin to study, tackle the

major points first. If you understand how whole chapters relate to one another then adding the smaller details will be easier.

10. Always focus on the bold print or italicized words in a text, as these are strong indicators of important material.

11. When you study consider using the same pen / pencil for all study related to this test and then take this pencil with you to the testing center. As you study play a mental trick on yourself by storing all the answers you write into your pencil. With that pencil with you at the exam, you have already written all the answers you are going to need. Sure it is a mental trick, but you have actually studied hard and written all the answers you are going to need. The mental trick simply serves as a psychological reminder to this fact.

12. Use flash cards. Sometimes there is information that simply must be devoted to memory (formulas, historical events, lists, vocabulary). For this type of information use flash cards. Three by five index cards work well. Put the definition or name of the formula on the front of the card and the answer on the back. Quiz yourself using the cards and reviewing the cards you missed in each set before attempting to work through the entire deck again. Flash cards work great for reviewing materials when you only have a few moments (perhaps between classes, or waiting in line).

13. Use mnemonic techniques to memorize materials. There are several mnemonic techniques that work well depending on the situation.
    a. For key words or lists consider using an ACRONYM to remember the list. An acronym is an invented combination of letters. If you have ever had the pleasure of playing a musical instrument you probably remember your grade school music teacher saying Every Good Boy Does Fine in an effort to help you remember the order of the notes on the clef scale.
    b. Another option for lists or key words is the ACROSTIC - You probably remember Please Excuse My Dear Aunt Sally from grade school when your teacher used it to help you remember the order of operations: Parenthesis, Exponents, Multiply, Divide, Addition, Subtraction.
    c. Location method – this method involves using a specific location to tie concepts together. For this example let us assume we are trying to memorize the following short list of landforms: hill, mountain, and plateau. We might picture our living room and imagine that as we walk in the door we are met immediately by a hill we must crawl over, followed by a television displaying a picture of the mountain. Lastly sitting there on the sofa is a plateau (you may even picture your uncle who has the flat buzz cut to help you remember the flat plateau). The more vivid you make the pictures the better and easier to remember them they will be.
    d. Rhyming Method – This is a two-step method in which you create words that rhyme with numbers and then build an association with those words. This method works best for ordered lists. For example if you were going to remember the following items for a grocery list: milk, bread, eggs, cheese, and chicken. To

remember the first item on the list we would find a word that rhymes with "one". For our case, we will choose "run". You are going to picture yourself running and carrying a gallon of milk. Much like the Location method, the trick to making this particular mnemonic device work is to make the picture and relationship between the two words as vivid as possible. So instead of just picturing yourself running with a gallon of milk in hand, you will picture yourself running while pouring the milk over your head. You could even get some of your other senses involved by imagining the smell of the milk to be putrid due to the hot weather in which you are running. By involving more senses and making the picture more vivid you are far less likely to forget the milk when you arrive at the store. This process would be repeated using the next number in the sequence and so on for each item that needs to be memorized.

14. Study groups – If you are a social learner then you will certainly benefit from the advantages that study groups offer. However, be prepared when you arrive and do not expect the study group to replace individual effort needed to learn new material. Study groups typically work best, for both social and solitary learners as a place to test knowledge. By quizzing one another, students can become more confident about material they know and find out what concepts may need a bit more attention. In addition, study groups can often help the student who is stumped on a particular concept. Do not be afraid to ask for study group members to explain something or help you understand it more clearly. Often hearing something described in different words is just the key our brain needs to unlock the information fully.

Scheduling Your Test

It may seem like a simplistic reminder, but if you are a morning person you will want to schedule your exam for the morning hours. Be sure to give yourself adequate time to get up, get ready and face any traffic on your way to the testing center. If you are better in the evenings, schedule the time that is near the end of the day but NOT the last session. Think back to elementary school and the fear of being the last person to turn in their test while others waited for you. You do not want the added stress of those around you leaving while you needlessly fear being the only person left.

Last Minute Preparation for Testing

You have studied as much as possible and tomorrow is the big day. What should you do tonight to make sure you are prepared for the big test? Let us begin with the one thing you should NOT do. Do not get caught up in cramming or even reviewing one last time. It is actually too late for that to do you much good. Tonight you should relax and focus on just a few items.

1. Get to bed early (or at least not excessively late) so you will be fresh for your test.

2. Use this time for positive self-talk. Remind yourself how much you have studied for

this exam and how prepared you are to show just how well you know the information.

3. The night before set out the items you will need for testing. Lay out clothing you plan to wear (go for comfort over style here). Make sure you include a jacket / hoodie as most testing centers tend to stay cold to help you stay awake. In addition, be sure your photo ID, pencils, calculator, and other requirements for the test are ready to be grabbed as you walk out the door.

4. Eat breakfast. Sure this is motherly advice, but it is good advice. Your brain needs fuel to function. Make sure you feed it. Avoid sugary foods that will leave you in a slump later and impact concentration levels. High protein foods are best as they help provide long-term energy.

5. Visit the restroom 15-20 minutes before the test and refrain from drinking fluids within an hour of your test.

6. Arrive 10-15 minutes early for the test so you do not have the stress of being late.

7. During the last few minutes, it is okay to review a formula or fact sheet of information you have dedicated to memory. One of the first things you will do when you sit for the exam, is to "dump" this information onto your scrap paper. Note that this is not the time to "cram" this information into your brain. It should already be memorized; you are just reviewing one last time.

8. Before you are seated for the exam, take a few deep breaths and relax. If you are subject to test anxiety we will cover more on how to relax a bit later.

Test-Taking Tips

When we began this text, we explained that taking a test was much like a sport and that understanding the rules of the game (test-taking skills) were just as important as ability to play (subject matter knowledge). In the next several pages we are going to explore ways you can put the rules of the game to work for you. By understanding and applying these test-taking strategies you improve your odds for success.

The number one tip for taking a test is to remain confident. It is amazing how confidence can change the outcome of situations. If you have studied adequately your hard work will pay off when it comes to taking the test. Just relax and trust yourself. If you suffer from test anxiety this tip is even more important. (See also the tips for test anxiety a few pages later.)

Once you begin the test and the timer begins, **take the first few moments to write down any formulas, dates, facts that you have dedicated to memory**, but are not included on a "fact sheet" for the exam. Doing this "brain dump" allows your brain to figuratively free up space that was being used to hold this information. It also ensures you do not forget the information later down the road when you need it.

Before you begin, take a look at the entire test and determine how you will **budget your time**. Often tests are computerized so this does not mean to click through every question, but simply learning how many questions there are so that you can stay on target to finish in the time allotted.

It often goes without saying, but it should not, that you need to **read the instructions**. You have probably had that teacher that gave you the following directions test that asked you to read the whole test before marking any answers and the result likely resulted in hilarity as your classmates did silly things because they didn't read the directions. (You would never fall for that trick yourself). While this is not elementary school and a standardized test is not going to set out to confuse you with directions, they are no less important. The difference between understanding mark the "best" answer and "only" answer can save you a great deal of confusion, and the difference between writing an essay about all of the topics or choosing a topic can mean the difference in passing and failing. So as elementary and boring as it is, take time to read the directions.

After reading the directions, you will want to **begin with the easiest questions first**. Most tests today are written in increased order of difficulty so this is typically the way you approach the test anyway. Answering easy questions will serve to boost your self-confidence and prepare you for the harder questions to come. However, if you encounter a problem that "stumps" you do not be afraid to leave it unanswered and return to it at a later time. Be sure you either mark the question on the test or make note on your scrap paper so you do not submit the test with an unanswered question. A question may often have clues to other questions within it.

As you answer questions **rely on your first impressions** and do not over think the answers. Unless you are 100% sure that you have the wrong answer and are 100% that the answer you are changing to is the correct answer do not deviate from your initial "gut reaction". Teachers would be quite wealthy if rewarded every time a student admitted to changing from a correct to incorrect answer. Do not be that student. Go with your first instincts unless you are absolutely sure you were wrong.

If you finish early, **use the time to review** your answers. Check to be sure you answered all of the questions. Proofread any essays for spelling and grammatical errors. If the test covered mathematics, check your calculations and use the calculator if it is acceptable to do so.

Multiple Choice Questions

Depending on the type of test you are likely to encounter different types of questions. Each of these question types has specific strategies that will help you in taking tests. The most common type of test question for standardized tests is the multiple-choice test. Consider these strategies for these types of questions:

1. Before reading the answers to a multiple-choice question try to formulate the answer on

your own. This adds confidence to your answer and ensures your brain is engaged in the answering process.

2. While you should formulate your own answer before reading the choices, be sure you read all of the answers before selecting your answer.

3. Statements that begin with concrete exceptions: never, none, always, except, most, least, are likely not the answer.

4. Eliminate unlikely answers. If you can reduce the possible answers to 2 you increase your odds of selecting the right answer or even guessing correctly.

5. If you must guess consider these guidelines:
    a. If there are two answers that are opposites from one another than the answer is likely one of those two answers.
    b. If there are two answers that are very similar, it is likely that the answer is neither of the two.
    c. Typically the longer and more descriptive answer is the correct answer
    d. If your answers are numbers then it is likely that the answer lies in the middle of the range of answers, not at the extremes. For example, if you answers are:
    a)   100   b)10   c) 9   d) 0.02
    You would eliminate the 100 and .02 and then determine if the answer is either 9 or 10. Again this is not always correct but helps in a situation where you may be forced to guess.

6. Be sure you answer every question. Most tests do not penalize you for guessing so it is best to answer every question even if guessing. Research your specific test for rules about penalties for wrong answers so you know how to approach guessing.

7. Watch out for questions that ask for opposites such as "which of the following is NOT" or "Which statement is false." These questions require reverse thinking.

True/False Questions

While it is not common for standardized tests to have questions other than multiple choice, sometimes you may encounter True/False questions. For True/False questions, consider the following tips:

1. Look at specific details. Specific details tend to make the statement true. For example, The Empire State Building is 1,250 feet tall. The detail of 1250 feet is a very specific detail and chances are this test question is TRUE.

2. When forced to guess, choose TRUE. More questions tend to be true than false, as most instructors and test writers find it more difficult to write statements that are false.

3. Look for extreme words such as: all, always, only, nobody, everybody, absolutely, etc. These words tend be used in statements that are FALSE.

4. Look for qualifying words such as: seldom, often, many, seldom, much, sometimes, etc. These words tend to make the statement TRUE.

5. Look for reasons. If the statement includes a reason it tends to be FALSE. Words like since, because, when, and if add justification or reasoning to the statement and tend to make it FALSE. Also check the justification to make sure it is complete. An incomplete justification makes the statement FALSE.

6. Look for negative words such as: not, none, or no. Also check for negative prefixes such as un-,im-, miss-. These negatives can confuse the statement and should be treated with caution.

Matching Questions

Sometimes you will encounter matching questions. These will often appear in a format very similar to multiple choice questions, but should be treated a bit differently. Here are a few tips to help you navigate these types of questions.

1. Read the directions carefully. Sometimes matching answers may be used only once, in other questions the answers may be used more than once. This certainly makes guessing much more difficult if there are answers that can be used more than once.

2. Look at both "sides" or sets of answers / questions. Get an idea of what the relationships might be between the two groups.

3. Use one list to find matches on the second list. This will keep confusion to a minimum.

4. Check the entire second "side" before selecting answers. There may be a more correct answer that follows.

5. Cross off matches on the second "side" in order to make finding subsequent matches easier.

6. Do not make a guess until you have worked through the entire first "side" one time completely.

Essay Questions

Some of the standardized test you will be taking may include essay questions. The approach to these tests is quite different from that of multiple choice or true-false exams as it is not really possible to guess at answers. When you answer essay questions you should remember that the idea is to show how well you both know the material and can explain it. You should also provide support for your answer. As you answer Essay Questions keep these tips in mind.

1. Read the entire question before beginning to write.

2. Construct a brief outline with the main points before you begin writing. If you are suffering from writers block then just begin by jotting down the ideas that come to mind. Even if you do not physically write out the outline, you should develop the main ideas in your head and have a distinct direction before you begin your writing.

3. Remember these tips for a good answer:
    a. Be direct in the answer to the question. Pose the answer in the first or second sentence of your answer.
    b. Make sure to include both general and specific information.
    c. Use vocabulary that is common to the course you are testing. If you are taking an ethics test, use the language of ethics.

4. Proofread your paper. Check for spelling, grammar, and punctuation. Also, make sure that your answer completely answers the question at hand and covers the entire problem. Be sure that your essay is easy to read and makes sense or flows well.

5. Monitor your time on an essay question. Time management is imperative in completion of the essay type question.

Overcoming Test Anxiety

One of the most debilitating problems a student can face is test anxiety. Test anxiety can manifest itself through tense muscles, fast heart and breathing rate, cramps, and even nausea. The student who suffers from test anxiety often knows the material as well as, or better than his or her classmates, but this never shows up on tests because the anxiety takes over. It is important for those who suffer from test anxiety to remain calm and confident. There are also other ways to help the brain and body cope with this type of anxiety.

1. **Breathe**. Breathing is not only essential to our existence, but serves as a way of relaxing the mind and body. Purposefully taking a few deep breaths can do a great deal to bring calm to the body. When you feel anxiety about to take over, begin to breathe deeply and calmly. Three to five deep breaths normally do the trick and can be repeated as often as necessary.

2. **Relax**. There will be times during the test that you begin to feel anxious. Recognize this feeling. Does it begin with tightening of the shoulders and neck or does it start in your stomach and slowly take over your body? Become aware of the feelings and the how they start. When you feel that trigger or beginning feeling consciously focus on

relaxation. There are many great books and websites dedicated to relaxation techniques. Explore and find one that works best for you.

3. **Take practice tests**. Before you sit for the actual exam, take as many practice exams as you can. Make the surroundings as much like the test center as you can. Give yourself the same time limits, and breaks you will be taking during the exam. The more you can make the practice seem like a test, the more the test will seem like practice. This brings us to the next point.

4. **Think of the test as practice**. This author, once had a student who scored a 32 on a quiz that covered multiplication facts all of which the student had recited the day before. It was apparent the student had become more and more anxious during the exam. As the class was assigned a new worksheet, this student was given the same quiz with one slight change made. At the top of the page, the word "Quiz" was replaced by "Practice". Guess what he made on the "Practice" sheet? You guessed it; he made a 100. Sure it is going to be hard to convince yourself that the test you are going to take at a testing center is really a "Practice" sheet, but there is no reason that you cannot retake the test. Most CLEP and standardized tests allow you to reset for the exam in 6 months (some less). Sure that is a while to wait and you do not want to stress over this test again, but remind yourself this is not the only shot you have at this. Take some of the pressure off of yourself.

5. **Do not panic**. Chances are that if you suffer from test anxiety you are already well acquainted with panic. Simply do not give into it. Force yourself to relax while reminding yourself of your confidence through positive self-talk.

6. **Stay positive**. Remind yourself of how much you are prepared for this and that a poor exam score only results from many missed questions not one or two.

7. **Stay realistic**. As we just mentioned one wrong answer does not mean you will fail the exam. Remind yourself that you simply need to pass. No one needs to know your score; you just need to do well enough to pass the exam. As you continue with positive self-talk do not let one or two questions send you into a spiral of self-doubt and more anxiety. Stay realistic about outcomes and your performance.

8. **Take care of yourself**. This is the most often overlooked advice when it comes to test anxiety. Your body is much more likely to respond appropriately if you are treating it appropriately by eating healthy foods and exercising regularly. In addition, regular exercise is shown to reduce stress and is a great way to build up tolerance and coping skills for test anxiety.

As you prepare for your upcoming exam, realized there are no shortcuts to doing well on a test. There is no replacement for knowledge of this subject matter, but hopefully the study skills mentioned here will help you make the most of your time spent studying. As you take the test remember the test- taking skills, as these will help you demonstrate your true mastery of the subject matter. Before you set for the exam and anxiety takes over be sure to put into practice some of the tactics we have mentioned for overcoming anxiety. If you already know what techniques work well for you those techniques will be at your disposal during the test.

Remember that just as the athlete must not only has mastery of the sport but must understand the rules and remain calm under pressure so must you the test-taker. It is important that you master all three skills as each plays a part in your success. You may not be scoring goals, sinking baskets, or serving aces, but you are going to win this game called test-taking. Just remember to have confidence in yourself.

Chapter 1: An Introduction to Sociology

What's the point?

- To define "sociology."
- To understand how sociology can be called a science.
- To understand what makes sociology a social science.
- To preview many of the terms and important figures found throughout this study of sociology.

What is Sociology?

As a social science, <u>sociology</u> is a systematic approach to thinking about, studying, and understanding society, human social behavior, and social groups. The topics discussed and studied within this field are as varied as the means sociologist use to study them. The broad expanse includes many different theories, methodologies, and areas of interest which this text will explore as fully as possible.

One important distinction to make note of when beginning a study of sociology is that its primary focus is groups. Social interactions are a favored observation as they are rife with examples of people interacting with others as members of groups.

The Sciences

To understand exactly how sociology fits into the realm of science, a definition of science should be examined. <u>Science</u> refers to any logical, systematic method by which knowledge can be acquired; it also refers to the actual body of knowledge produced by such methods. All sciences can be differentiated into one or two prevailing types:
- The <u>natural sciences</u>: referring to the study of physical and biological phenomena.
  - Typically more objective findings.
- The <u>social sciences</u>: referring to the study of various aspects of human behavior.
  - Typically more subjective findings.

Within both schools of scientific thought, the assumption is held that an underlying order in the universe exists. Scientists commonly search for predictable generalizations that can not only be applied to specific organisms but also to others of that type of organism.

Social Sciences

As a discipline, Sociology is less advanced than most of the other social and natural sciences. The main reason is the subject matter. Studying human social behavior with scientific methods is often challenging; subjects being studied typically know they are being studied and thus alter their behaviors. Altered behaviors lead to altered results.

The other social sciences greatly impact the study of sociology and vice versa.

Anthropology:

Anthropology is the study of human evolution and culture that focuses on small-scale, primitive societies. In contrast, Sociology focuses more exclusively on groups in modern industrial societies. The various branches of anthropology include: archaeology (study of material remains from past cultures), linguistics (study of human speech), physical anthropology (using fossils to trace human evolution), cultural anthropology (study of pre-modern ways of life), history (study of causes and meanings of past events), and human ecology (study of relationships between organisms and their environment).

Sociologists use anthropological reports, called ethnography, to compare past societies with modern societies.

Economics:

Economics is the study of production, distribution, and consumption of goods and services. Economists attempt to explain and predict human behavior as it relates to economic forces and has developed quite sophisticated mathematical analyses to do so. Sociologists realize that economic and material concerns influence society's behavior.

Psychology:

Psychology is the study of mental processes and perception in individuals. In contrast, sociology focuses on groups of individuals.

The two fields do share one particular sub-field of study: social psychology, the study of how personality and behavior are influenced by social elements.

Political Science:

Political science is the study of political power, political processes, and governmental systems. This field of study is based in two areas: politics and government, and it explores the relationship between them.

Political sociology is a developing branch of study that is influencing political scientists. Considering political behavior, political sociology is the study of social interaction involved in the process of government. Sociologists are more interested in the relationships between political and social institutions.

All of the social sciences, therefore, influence one another and scientists in each category can glean helpful information from other fields of study to help their own specialty.

Chapter Previews

The remainder of Chapter 1 contains a comprehensive listing of important figures, theories, and terms. The terms are organized alphabetically, according to the chapter in which they appear.

This list can be utilized before, during, and after an in-depth study of the material in this book:

- Before: An overview of terms and definitions will develop a familiarity with the concepts.
- During: Using the listing as a glossary of sorts throughout the study of this material, will assist the student retain important definitions.
- After: The listings can be used as a self-test after completion of each chapter and at the end of the book.

Chapter 2 Preview

When reading about the Sociological Perspective in Chapter 2, the following terms are important to know and understand:

Term	Definition
Academic (Indirect) Sociology	Research methodology with the purpose of discovering knowledge for the sake of obtaining knowledge.
Applied (Direct) Sociology	Research methodology with the purpose of finding solutions to practical problems.
Case Study	Research method that involves a detailed record of an event, group, or social process – past or present.
Causation	The identification of one variable influencing another.
Chicago School	The first educational institution to offer a doctoral degree in Sociology.
Community School	Research method that involves collecting massive amounts of data concerning a small area that provides enough information to understand the community.
Comparative Analysis	Comparing multiple systems or structures from different points in time.
Conflict Perspective	View of sociology that focuses on the struggles of a society that result from tension, competition, and change.
Control Group	A group in sociological experimentation that is not exposed to the independent variable.
Dependent Variable	The variable of the sociological experimentation that is likely to change as the independent variable does.
Experimental Group	The group in a sociological experiment that is exposed to the independent variable.

Functionalist Perspective	The viewpoint of sociology that sees society as a whole consisting of various parts, each of which have unique and necessary functions.
Hawthorne Effect	When a subject's assumptions about an experiment affect the experiment's results – either positively or negatively.
Independent Variable	The variable that is introduced (or used in differing amounts) in an effort to elicit a change in the dependent variable.
Interactionist Perspective	The viewpoint in sociology that considers how the parts of society act and react.
Interview Technique	Research method that involves the researcher asking the subject questions.
Latent Function	An unintended consequence.
Manifest Function	An obvious consequence.
Methodology	A set of standards and procedures that guide experimentation and observation.
Nonparticipant Observation	The type of observation where the researchers stays out of the action.
Objectivity	Based in calculable data or other non-personal information.
Participant Observation	Research method that involves a researcher annotating observations as they occur.
Population	The tested or observed group of individuals.
Population Sample	A selection of test subjects that is representative of the entire population.
Qualitative Methods	Use descriptions and shy away from hard facts and toward perception-based information.
Quantitative Methods	Use quantifiable measurements like numbers and statistics.
Questionnaire Technique	Interview technique that uses a standard form that respondents fill out and return.
Random Sample	A selection of test subjects chosen in a random manner; it is usually representative if a large enough sample is taken.
Replication	Repeating a study or experiment to verify results.
Research Evaluation	Research method that involves making use of information already available from various sources.
Respondents	Tested individuals; test subjects.
Sociological Concept	Generalization based on data.
Social Darwinism	Survival of the fittest society.
Social Dynamics	The study of a society's ability to adapt to changes, both internal and external.
Social Experiment	Research method in which two variables are observed in a carefully controlled environment; the relationship between the variables is determined.
Social Statistics	The study of order and stability in society.
Sociology	Systematic approach to thinking about, studying, and understanding society, human social behavior, and social

	groups.
Structured	An inflexible interview technique; each subject is asked the same questions in the same order and must reply from a set of predetermined possible answers.
Subjectivity	Based on values or experiences.
Survey	A systematic and standardized means of collecting data.
Symbol	Anything that represents something else.
Symbolic Interaction	How people react to items within a society.
Theoretical Perspective	Broad assumptions about society and social behavior that provides a point of view for the study of specific problems.
Theory	An organized statement that establishes a set of concepts in a relevant way to explain a possible relationship among them.
Unobtrusive Measures	An attempt made by researchers to study individuals without imposing themselves on them.
Unstructured	A form of interviewing where the subjects are asked open-ended questions.
Variable	One part of an experiment that is subject to change.

When reading through Chapter 2, the following people are important:

Sociologist	Information
Comte, Auguste	(1798-1857) Founder of sociology. Coined the term "sociology."
Durkheim, Emile	(1858-1917) Believed societies unified by shared values and beliefs
Mark, Karl	(1818-1883) Influential in many scientific circles. Writings inspired the Socialist and Communist movements.
Spencer, Herbert	(1820-1903) Applied Darwin's evolutionary theory to societies in order to explain social order and change.
Weber, Max	Most influential Western sociologist; German.

The following charts or tables illustrate important information pertinent to Chapter 2 material:

- Four types of suicide as explained by Emile Durkheim:
  - Egotistic: Victim does not feel connected to the large society.
  - Altruistic: Victim places welfare of other above own life.
  - Fatalistic: Victim feels powerless to regulate his or her own life.
  - Anomic: Victim response to social disorder.

- The common perspectives of sociological study and the sociologists associated with them:

Perspective	Supporting Sociologists	Explanations
Functionalist	Spencer, Durkheim, Parsons, and Merton	-Society consists of several parts. -Each part has specific functions. -Each function is necessary to society's stability.
Conflict	Marx, Mills, Dahrendorf, and Collins	-Society changes through conflict. -Those struggles erupt in all types of groups and dynamics. -Those struggles can be positive.
Interactionist	Weber, Mead, Goffman, Homans	-Society is made up of people who interact daily. -Individuals are constantly developing their society by their daily actions and reactions.

Chapter 3 Preview

When reading about social processes in Chapter 3, the following terms are important to know and understand:

Term	Definition
Achieved Status	Social status that one earns.
Agents of Socialization	The influences that affect individuals through the lifespan.
Aggregate	People located in the same place at the same time; not considered a group.
Anomie	A state of confusion or imbalance that exists when norms are weak, absent, or conflicting.
Ascribed Status	Social status with which one is born.
Basic Drives	Urges that push a person to fulfill basic needs.
Beliefs	Shared ideas collectively held by those within a culture.
Bereavement	The process of dealing with the loss of a loved one.
Bureaucracy	Hierarchical authority structure with strict rules and procedures.
Collective Organization	Formal association consisting of part-time volunteers who contribute to many of the necessary aspects of an organization, including decision-making.
Counterculture	A culture within a culture that has norms, values, and lifestyles in

	complete opposition to those of the dominant culture.
Crime	An act that contradicts the law and is punishable by negative sanctions.
Culture -Material Culture -Nonmaterial Culture	Complex system developed to define a society's way of life; includes the product of a society, material and non-material. -Physical objects created and valued by members of a society. -Abstract, intangible human creations.
Cultural Ecology	A theory that states that culture is formed by the limitations or excess of resources and other changes in the environment.
Cultural Integration	The tendency toward certain mores, values, and beliefs even among the diversity within a society.
Cultural Relativism	The idea that another culture cannot be judged by the standards of another.
Cultural Universals	Similar norms found in almost every society.
Determinate Task	A task that has a definite single answer.
Deviance	Behavior that violates social norms and expectations; usually results in the disapproval of a large number of people.
Dramaturgical Approach	Analyzes social interactions as if the participants are acting out a play or scene.
Dyad	A two-member group.
Ecological Approach	Analyzes the entire environment as it correlates to society and culture.
Ecology	The study of the relationship between various organisms and their environments.
Ethnocentrism	Belief that one's own culture is the 'right' or 'normal' one.
Ethnomethodology	Analyzes how people uses commonly understood rules of engagement to dictate how they react to specific situations and thereby be understood by all involved.
Goal Displacement	When individuals in a bureaucracy take their focus off the overall goals of the organization.
Group	Two or more people who share common ideas, feeling, and pursuits, and who interact frequently and intimately.
Group Conformity	Individuals acting for the good of the group instead of themselves.
Group Polarization	The tendency of a group to make more extreme decisions than each member would on their own.
Groupthink	When a group attempts to reach a conclusion without researching or testing various sides.
Habits	Repetitive patterns of behavior.
Ideal Culture	The established standard of norms and values.
Ideologies	Cultural beliefs that justify one group's goals.
Impression Management	Attempting to manage the impressions others make by creating scenes.
Incest Taboo	Powerful moral prohibition against sexual relations among close relatives.

Indeterminate Task	A task that does not have an absolute answer.
Institution	Collection of shared expectations about long-held public habits.
Language	Written and spoken forms of human speech.
Leader	Someone who is able to influence the behavior of others primarily due to their personality traits.
Master Class	A person's most significant social status.
Mental Disorder	A psychological inability to handle ordinary situations.
Nonverbal Communication	The exchange of information via non-linguistic means or symbols.
Norms	Guidelines that establish the accepted behavior in given situations.
Oligarchy	An organization that is ruled by a hierarchy with a few powerful individuals at the top.
Organization	Large, formal association.
Parkinson's Law	The idea that in a bureaucracy, the workload tends to expand to fill the time allotted for it.
Personality	The patterns of thought, feeling, and action of an individual.
Peter Principle	The idea that in a hierarchy, every employee tends to rise (or rather fall) to his level of incompetence.
Primary Group	A group made up of individuals who know each other more intimately and interact more frequently.
Psychosis	A profound mental disturbance or break with reality that renders the individual unable to function appropriately in society.
Real Culture	The actual norms and values practiced inside a society.
Resocialization	Process of learning a new set of socially acceptable behaviors while dropping previously acquired learned behaviors.
Role	Established pattern of behavior, associated with a set of obligations or privileges.
Role Conflict	The problem that results when two or more roles contradict each other.
Role Confusion	Experienced when a single person has several social statuses, each with different roles.
Role Expectations	Social norms attributed to a certain role.
Role Performance	Actual behavior exhibited by someone in a role.
Role Set	Many related roles.
Role Strain	The problem of too many expectations being inherent in one role.
Sanctions	Rewards for conformity and punishments for nonconformity.
-Informal Sanctions	-Disapproval or rejection imposed by a primary group for nonconformity.
-Formal Sanctions	-Punishments enacted by organizations.
Secondary Group	A group that interacts on a short-term, less personal basis.
Simple Reflexes	Involuntary muscle responses.
Small Group	Contains few members who all relate to one another as individuals.
Social Category	People who are connected by an ideal, but who lack social structure. Not considered a group.

Social Class	Group of individuals who have the same status within a society.
Social Control	Measures taken to encourage conformity and discourage or restrain deviance.
Social Institution	Established set of roles, statuses, and groups, all of which share common norms and values that have developed out of social need.
Social Interaction	The process of people reacting and responding to one another in society.
Social Network	A loosely unified group of people whose members interact on occasion and who share a loose sense of identity.
Social Order	The state a society is in when most of its members are in a state of conformity to the established norms.
Social Psychology	Analyzes how personality and behavior is influenced or altered by social contexts.
Social Structure	The pattern of interacting relationships among the different components of the society.
Socialization	The process by which individuals learn the roles and structure of their society.
Society	People who share a culture, live in the same physical territory, and are under the same authority or political entity.
Status	A person's position in a society.
Status Inconsistency	A contradictory set of statuses applied to one person.
Stigma	A characteristic much like a 'mark' that is shared by deviants and sets them apart from 'normal' members of society.
Subcultures	A culture within a culture whose norms, values, and lifestyles differ in some way from those of the dominant culture.
Symbol	Agreed upon representation of something else.
Symbolic Interaction	How symbols, like signs, gestures, and language, make it possible for people to interact.
Triad	A three-member group.
Universals	Characteristics shared by many cultures.
Values	Shared ideas of what is good, right, and desirable.

The following portions of important information are found in Chapter 3:

- The three types of social norms:
  1. Folkways: Ordinary, everyday conventions of life.
  2. Mores: Stronger, more morally significant norm.
  3. Law: A standard that is formally enacted by political authority.

- The three processes that lead to cultural change:
  1. Discovery: An increase in knowledge or insight.
  2. Invention: The new use of existing knowledge to create something that previously did not exist.
  3. Diffusion: The spread of cultural elements from one culture to another.

- The three components of personality:
  1. Cognitive component: Thoughts, beliefs, perceptions, and other intellectual abilities.
  2. Emotional aspect: Feelings.
  3. Behavioral component: Skills, aptitudes, competencies.

- The three broadest types of organizations:
  1. Voluntary: People are free to join and leave as they become interested in the group's purposes.
  2. Utilitarian: Members join such organizations for practical reasons, usually for some gain.
  3. Coercive: Individuals are forced to participate.

- Each formal organization has the following:
  - Informal structure: Personal interactions between members, improving the efficiency of the organization.
  - Organizational culture: Important to success, the well-defined identity, clear values, heroes, rites and rituals bring order to the work of the organization.
  - Cultural network: Hidden hierarchy that obtains and spreads information.

Chapter 4 Preview

When reading about social stratification in Chapter 4, the following terms are important to know and understand:

Term	Definition
Absolution Deprivation	An inability to provide basic sustenance.
Affirmative Action	A set of policies that grant preferences to minorities in an effort to make up for past discrimination.
Ageism	The belief that one age strata are inferior to another and that this difference justifies unequal treatment.
Caste System	A stratification method in which placement is determined by birth (ascribed status).
Class	A portion of people who share common relationships and means of production or sources or wealth.

Class Consciousness	Awareness of common class interests.
Class Divisions	Real and/or perceived differences between classes.
Closed System	A social stratification method where ascribed statuses are the primary labeling mechanism and where there is very little change of changing status.
Culture of Poverty	Set of values and norms common to the poor subculture.
Discrimination	Unequal treatment, usually negative or limiting, of individuals based on their race, ethnicity, or other group membership.
Endogamy	Marrying within the same social caste.
False Consciousness	Perception of class reality is not consistent with situational reality.
Gender	Culturally learned differences between males and females and socially learned traits of each.
Gender Identity	One's self-concept of being male or female.
Gender Roles	Socially acceptable behaviors of each sex.
Ideology	A set of beliefs that helps to explain the arrangement of society.
Institutional Discrimination	Unequal treatment based on long-standing social custom or routine.
Institutional Racism	Policies that appear to be racially neutral but actually limit opportunities for minority groups.
Internal Colonialism	An economic exploitation in which the dominant group places minorities as subordinates for cheap labor.
Legal Discrimination	Unequal treatment upheld by law.
Minority Groups	A group that consists of people who share physical attributes or cultural practices that are different from the main culture and this difference makes them susceptible to unusual or unequal treatment.
Open System	A social stratification method where achieved statuses are the primary labeling mechanism and where there is greater likelihood of influencing social status.
Prejudice	A rigid, irrational attitude toward a group of people based on racial or ethnic differences.
Racism	The belief that one ethnicity or race is inferior to another, justifying unequal treatment.
Relative Deprivation	An inability to maintain a standard of living that compares to the customary societal level.
Ritual Pollution	Contact between members of different social castes.
Sex	Biologically distinctive categories of humans.
Sexism	The belief that one sex is inferior to another and that difference justifies unequal treatment.
Social Gerontology	The study of the social aspects of aging
Social Inequality	Treatment that differs according to age, sex, race, religion,

	sexual orientation, or education; often social rewards are not equally shared.
Social Mobility	The upward or downward movement from one social class to another.
Social Status	A socially defined position, or ranking; a society's stratification system.
Social Consistency	The tendency of people who rank high in one social area to also rank high in another.
Status Inconsistency	The occurrence of a person ranking high in one social area but low in another.
Status Symbol	Objects or speech patterns that are easily recognized as associated with a certain status.

The following portions of information are found in Chapter 4. They are provided here as a study tool.

- Types of social movement:
  - Upward mobility: Aided by industrial development and education; seen as a product of geographic mobility and urbanization.
  - Downward mobility: Caused by a lack of those things that lead to upward mobility, like formal education.
  - Horizontal mobility: Involves a social change while retaining the same social status.
  - Intergenerational mobility: How an individual's status compares to his or her parents'.
  - Intragenerational mobility: How an individual's status changes during the course of his or her life.
  - Structural mobility: Caused by changes in the economy and not due to individual achievement.
  - Exchange mobility: Occurs when people at different hierarchical levels exchange places.

- The three methods used to analyze American class structure:
  - Reputation method: Asking how members of the society view the stratification.
  - Subjective method: Asking of which class members of a society believe they are a part.
  - Objective method: Ranks people based on facts like income and occupation.

- Characteristics of the culture of poverty:
  - Inability to resist impulsive gratification.
  - Suspicious of all authority.
  - Lacking in a plan for the future.
  - Having a sense of resignation.

- Minority group traits:
  - Culturally determined traits: Dress, language, and hairstyle.
  - Biologically determined traits: Skin color and hair texture.

- Five minority group properties:
  1. Exploited by (or suffer damages from) the dominant group.
  2. Identified by at least one socially visible characteristic.
  3. Share a common identity and share a strong sense of solidarity.
  4. Born into the group. (i.e. They are members due to an ascribed status.)
  5. Marry within the group (usually).

- Five ways minority groups influence the dominant society:
  1. Passive acceptance: Minorities accept the current situation.
  2. Aggression: Expressions of dissatisfaction, verbal, written, or physical violence.
  3. Collective protest: Minorities band together to express dissatisfaction.
  4. Self-segregation: Voluntary separation from the dominant society.
  5. Voluntary assimilation: Attempting to blend into the dominant society by learning the culture.

- Sources of prejudice:
  - Stereotype: An exaggerated, and usually unfavorable, belief about a group of people. Every member of the group is assumed to have those traits.
  - Authoritarian personality: Traits of a prejudiced thinker (conformity, intolerant, and insecure).
  - Irrationality: Illogical, irrational, or inconsistent beliefs about groups of people.
  - Scapegoating: Projecting blame onto another person or group who is powerless to stop the threat.
  - Social environment: Either encourages or discourages prejudicial behavior. Social environments that encourage prejudice include competitions, inequality, and minimal contact between members.

- Three reasons for workplace inequality:
  1. Human capital model: Men and women contribute unequally to the labor market and invest in training and education unequally. This is commonly attributed to women's lack of desire to expend more energy outside their home/families.
  2. Considered choice model: Women choose lower-end jobs that require less from them because of their family/home commitments.
  3. Discrimination model: Women are commonly placed in jobs that lack equal wages or promotion opportunity. These types of jobs are commonly called "pink-collar" jobs and consist of such placements as waitress, cashier, and receptionist.

- Three processes of aging:
  1. Physical aging: The body changes that accompany maturation.
  2. Psychological aging: Personality changes.
  3. Social aging: Transitions between social statuses.

- Four perspectives of social gerontology:
  1. Disengagement theory: The elderly withdraw from society (and society withdraws from the elderly). Social roles diminish, leading many to depression.
  2. Activity theory: The elderly reduce their levels of activity and involvement due to societal structures, but if they can maintain some of their activity level, they feel better about themselves.
  3. Continuity theory: The elderly are simply continuing their life journey and will tend to deal with the changes at this stage similar to how they dealt with change throughout their life.
  4. Aged as a subculture: The elderly, feeling separate from other age groups, seek to spend their time with others of the same subculture.

Chapter 5 Preview

When reading about social institutions in Chapter 5, the following terms are important to know and understand:

Term	Definition
Authority	Legitimate Power.
Blended Family	A family pattern consisting of children from both parents' previous marriages.
Capitalism	An economic system in which the means of production are privately owned and distributed competitively in the hopes of making a profit.
Coercion	Forcing a person to obey someone who is exerting illegitimate power.
Cohabitation	Living together without a legal marriage.

Community Ownership	An entire community owns property and any member can use it.
De Facto Segregation	Segregation based on geographic area.
De Jure Segregation	Segregation upheld by law.
Disease	A condition that is objectively diagnosed by a medical practitioner, usually of biological origin.
Division of Labor	How work is divided between individuals and groups who are specialized in particular activities.
Economy	The system for producing, distributing, and consuming goods and services in a society.
Epidemiology	The study of the origin, distribution, and transmission of a disease in the population.
Extended Family	A family pattern consisting of more than two generations living as a unit either under one roof or in close proximity.
Family	Relatively permanent group of individuals who are related by ancestry, marriage, or adoption who also live together and take care of young.
Health	The absence of disease and the ability to respond effectively to the environment.
Illness	A condition where an individual perceives that he/she is suffering a bodily disorder; psychological origin.
Interest Groups	Organizations that seek to influence government policies and public opinion.
Kinship	A network of families who are related by common ancestry, adoption, marriage, or affiliation.
Lobbying	Attempting to persuade a political decision-maker.
Magnet Schools	Inner-city schools that offer specialized programs to encourage middle-class suburban students to attend.
Majority-to-Minority Transfer	A free transportation program that helps students move from a school where they are a majority to one where they are a minority.
Mechanical Solidarity	The bond of those in a society who share similar workloads and experiences.
Nuclear Family	A family pattern consisting of a couple and their children.
Organic Solidarity	The bond of those in a society who are interdependent on one another's differences.
Political Institutions	Enduring social arrangements that distribute

	and exercise power.
Political Order	The institutionalized system from which individuals or groups exert power over others.
Political Party	Organizations made up of people with similar beliefs whose aim is to gain legitimate control over government.
Political Processes	Part of governments that grant rights and freedoms to citizens, assign responsibilities, and control access to and use of resources.
Politics	The social process by which people and groups acquire, exercise, maintain and/or lose power over others.
Power	The ability to control or influence the actions and behaviors of others, with or without their consent.
Private Ownership	When an individual owns property.
Property	The set of rights an owner has versus those of others who do not own it.
Public Ownership	When the state or political authority owns the property on behalf of the population.
Reconstituted Family	A family pattern that includes children from one of the parent's previous marriages.
Religiosity	The nature and level of personal religious experiences.
Secularization	The process of religion losing its influence on society.
Sickness	A condition where others observe that an individual is suffering a bodily disease; sociological origin.
Single-Parent Family	Households with only one parent.
Social Solidarity	The extent members of a society are bound together.
Socialism	An economic system in which the means of production are controlled and distributed by the state.

The following sections provide specialized study aids for each of the topics covered in this section. Review each carefully before, during, and after reading the material to ensure your success.

Concerning Family Institutions
Functionalists consider the four basic functions that the family performs for society: socialization, affection & companionship, sexual regulation, and economic cooperation.

Conflict theorists consider the family to be the primary institution in which male dominance is propagated; in the family, benefits are not equally distributed.

- The two types of families:
  1. Family of orientation: The family into which an individual is born. This offers the most opportunities for socialization.
  2. Family of procreation: The family that individuals create by marrying and having children.

- Conditions that increase the likelihood of divorce:
  - The couple married young.
  - The couple married after a short courtship.
  - The couple lives in an urban setting.
  - Friends/relatives of the couple disapprove of the union.

- Reasons for marital breakdown:
  - Stress on the nuclear family.
  - Ending of romantic love, if not followed or shifted to rational love.
  - Changed role of women can threaten the stability of the male's ideal.
  - Sexual permissiveness takes the trust of the couple and shatters it.

- Factors leading to remarriage failure:
  - Step-parenting problems.
  - Carrying over problems from first marriage into second.
  - Reacting quicker to signs of marital problems.
  - Ease of getting a divorce.

- The three types of residential living:
  1. Patrilocal residence: Custom dictates that married partners dwell in or near the husband's father.
  2. Matrilocal residence: Custom dictates that married partners dwell in or near the wife's father.
  3. Neolocal residence: Custom dictates that married partners dwell in a new residence separate from the kin of either spouse.

- Types of marital authority:
  1. Patriarchy: Husband has more authority in the family.
  2. Matriarchy: Wife has more authority in the family.
  3. Egalitarian: Husband and wife share authority equally in the family.

- Systems of inheritance and family descent:
  1. Patrilineal system: Descent and inheritance passes through the male side of the family.
  2. Matrilineal system: Descent and inheritance passes through the female side of the family.
  3. Bilateral system: Descent and inheritance passes through both sides of the family.

Concerning Educational Institutions:

Functionalists view schools as important to maintaining social order with the five main functions being: socialization, social control, selection & allocation, assimilation of newcomers, and social innovation and change.

Conflict theorists view schools as a tool used by different social groups to maintain or get wealth, power, and prestige by helping to reproduce the class system within each new generation.

- The three subcultures of students:
  1. Academic: Intellectual leaders, high grades, academic activities.
  2. Fun: Popular students, social, athletics/parties/dating.
  3. Delinquent: Rebellious toward authority, rules, and/or structure.

- The five intended functions of education:
  1. Socialization: The culturally-based transmission of knowledge, technical skills, values, and norms.
     i. Geography, math, science, communication along with politics, behavior, morality, and heritage.
  2. Social control: Teaching culturally appropriate behavior, cooperation, loyalty, and obedience.
  3. Selection and allocation: Screening and selection for different types of jobs through diplomas and certifications.
  4. Assimilation: Social integration of minorities into the dominant society through the teaching of the English language, patriotism, US history, customs, and traditions.
  5. Innovation and change: Develops new knowledge and skills to add to the cultural heritage. Education stimulates intellectual curiosity and provides opportunity for research and experimentation.
     i. Basic research: Systematic inquiry concerned with establishing new knowledge by uncovering basic aspects.

ii.   Applied research: Experimenting with practical uses of existing knowledge.

Concerning Religious Institutions:

Functionalists believe that religion promotes social stability and the status quo through rituals and value reinforcement.

Conflict theorists consider religion as a tool of the powerful.

- The four types of religion:
  1. Animatism: Belief system based on the existence of a spirit or force found within people, animals, plants, or inanimate objects and which contains personality and will, but no soul.
  2. Animism: Belief system based on the existence of a spirit or force found in everything within nature and which contains a soul.
  3. Theism: Belief system based on one or more supreme beings or gods who deserve to be worshipped because of their power and influence.
      i.   Monotheism: Belief system based on the existence of one supreme god.
      ii.   Polytheism: Belief system based on the existence of more than one god.
  4. Ethical religions: Belief system based on philosophical ideals and how to achieve them.

- Four types of religious organizations:
  1. Ecclesia: Large, formally organized religious body that is considered the national or official religion. All members of a society belong to this body. An ecclesia wields influence over the government. Ecclesias are not common today, but some organizations roughly approximate them.
  2. Denomination: Also known as a church, it is a well-established and socially accepted religious organization. Believers fall into the hierarchy and conform to doctrines and rituals. Denominations are usually tolerant of each other and are not officially linked to state or government.
  3. Sect: Sects are small and less formally organized. They have split from a denomination and in some way protest against the parent religion. They are generally uncompromising and indifferent or hostile toward government.
  4. Cult: Loosely organized religious movement with ideas that are in direct opposition to established and accepted religious traditions.

Concerning Political Institutions:

Functionalists conclude that the emergence of the state is in direct response to the service it provides in maintaining the social system.

Conflict theorists assert that the state exists only to safeguard the interest of the privileged few.

- The three means of control:
  1. Reward: Offering a benefit or something positive in exchange for obedience or compliance.
  2. Punishment: Threatening or creating negative consequences for disobedience.
  3. Influence: Manipulating information, attitudes, and feelings.

- The two types of power:
  1. Illegitimate: Few in society view the people who are acting in power do not have a right to do so.
  2. Legitimate: Society views the power or authority to be valid and/or justified.

- The three types of legitimate power:
  1. Traditional: Power is based on socially accepted customs and practices. It has historical roots and is religiously sanctioned; for these reasons, it is usually hereditary and an ascribed status. Leadership quality is not a requirement; people will obey because they always have.
  2. Rational-legal: Power is based on rules, regulations, and procedures that are expressly designed to establish power and how it is exercised and distributed. It is based more on the position and not the person holding the position.
  3. Charismatic: Power is based on the qualities of the leader, like being able to excite and inspire his/her followers. It is often unstable as it rests with the charisma of one person. This kind of leader can have a positive or negative influence on societies.

- The three perspectives on the distribution of political power:
  - Pluralist: Social order is achieved when the state effectively mediates interest groups, seeks public consensus, and passes laws and regulations to reflect that consensus.
  - Elitist: Democracies in the modern world are led by a very small minority (the elite).
  - Class conflict: Derived from Karl Marx's works, this perspective believes that power is in the hands of a small ruling class.

- The three most common types of government:
  1. Authoritarianism: Form of government where rulers rarely consider what the public wants.
  2. Totalitarianism: Form of government where rulers don't recognize any limits to their authority.
  3. Democracy: Form of government based on participation of the population.

- The three main types of democracy:
  1. True: All citizens have direct participation in government.
  2. Representative: Citizens can vote for leaders to represent them in government. There is no guarantee that those representatives will act as their constituents would want.
  3. Liberal: Supports the protections of individual rights.

- The three types of political activity:
  1. Gladiatorial: Those who hold office, campaign actively, and in other ways have a high-level of involvement.
  2. Transitional: Those who attend meetings and contact officials.
  3. Spectator: Those who have little involvement, perhaps voting and displaying a bumper sticker.

- Types of special interest groups:
  - Public interest groups: Their goal is to represent the public good.
  - Single-issue groups: They concentrate on one narrowly defined interest.
  - Industry groups: Their goal is to represent large organizations.
  - Political Action Committees (PACs): They aim to garner political influence by making political contributions.

Concerning Medical Institutions:
Functionalists relate sickness to a form of deviance that society attempts to overcome.

Conflict theorists concentrate on the assumptions that good health is a highly prized resource and the fact that it is unequally distributed among society's members.

- Types of disease:
  - Endemic: A disease that is always present in a population.
  - Epidemic: A usually uncommon disease that becomes a rapidly wide-spreading outbreak that affects a significant portion of the population.
  - Pandemic: A disease that has spread worldwide.
  - Acute: A disease that onsets rapidly and has a short duration.
  - Chronic: A disease that onsets slowly and has a long duration.

Concerning Economic Institutions:
- Key elements of capitalism:
  - Private Property Ownership
  - Profit
  - Competition

- The drawbacks of capitalism:
  - Inflation (increasing cost of goods and services)
  - Social inequality (those who own and those who do not)
  - Large poverty class (those who have can succeed, but possibly not those who don't)
  - Unemployment (a continual need)
  - Stagflation (unemployment combined with inflation)

Chapter 6 Preview

When reading about social patterns in Chapter 6, the following terms are important to know and understand:

Term	Definition
Concentric Zone Model	States that cities grow outward in a series of concentric circles that radiate outward from the business center.
Demography	The study of population.
Emigrants	People who move out of a country.
Fecundity	The potential number of children the average healthy woman can bear.
Fertility	The number of children the average woman is bearing in a society.
Immigrants	People who move into a country.
Infant Mortality Rate	The number of deaths per 1,000 infants under one year of age.
Life Expectancy	The number of years a population's newborn is expected to live.
Lifespan	The maximum possible number of years a species can live.
Megalopolis	Two or more major metropolitan areas linked politically, economically, socially, or geographically.
Metropolis	An economic and geographic region consisting of a central city and its suburbs.
Neonatal Mortality Rate	The number of deaths per 1,000 infants under one month of age.
Overurbanization	A condition that occurs when a population exceeds the ability of the society's resources.
Population Composition	The characteristics of a population; the number and type of people.
Population Growth Rate	The difference between the number of people added to population and the number of people subtracted from a population and expressed as an annual percentage.

Suburbs	Residential area on the outskirts of a central city.
Urbanism	The study of the cultural and social characteristics of cities.
Urbanization	The movement of people from rural to urban areas.

The following information contains highlights of important information from Chapter 6. Study it carefully!

- The three variables of demographic study:
    1. Birth rate: The number of births per 1,000 women in a population per year.
    2. Death rate: The number of deaths per 1,000 members of the population per year. The death rate, or mortality, of a society varies by social class.
    3. Migration: The movement of people from one place to another, into or out of a society.

- Two factors affecting birth rate:
    1. Biological factors: the number of women actually of childbearing age and the health of those women.
    2. Social factors: the type of birth control methods available in the society.

- The two types of migration:
    1. International migration: Movement from one country to another.
    2. Internal migration: Movement within a country.

- Factors affecting migration:
    - Push factors: Reasons that push people out of a country or region, like overpopulation, horrid climate, and inadequate housing and/or employment opportunities.
    - Pull factors: Reasons that attract people to a country or region, like political or religious freedoms, pleasant weather, employment opportunities, etc.

- The three characteristics of a city:
    1. Size: May leave individuals feeling lost and anonymous.
    2. Population density: Forces individuals into specific interactions (not whole relationships).
    3. Social diversity: Opens individuals to different viewpoints and cultures.

Chapter 7 Preview

When reading more about social processes in Chapter 7, the following terms are important to know and understand:

Term	Definition
Collective Behavior	Spontaneous actions of people trying to work out common responses to ambiguous situations that are unpredictable, unstructured, and unstable.
Convergence Theory	The idea that all societies are becoming more similar due to modernization.
Crowds	Temporary groups of people who are in close proximity to one another and who have a common focus.
Cultural Lag	The delay that exists between a technological development and the cultivation of an adequate cultural understanding and interaction with it.
Mass Behavior	A widely dispersed crowd that does not have face-to-face contact, but who still influences one another indirectly through common sources of information.
Modernization	The process of economic, cultural, and social change that must occur for a society to transform into an industrial society.
Revolution	A violent overthrow of an existing social system or political authority.
Social Movement	A large group of people joined together to bring about or resist a social or cultural change.
Sociocultural Evolution	The tendency for social structures to become more complex over time.
Technological Determinism	The idea that available technology determines a society's culture, social structure, and history.
Technology	The practical application of knowledge.
Terrorism	Violent use of force against civilians to intimidate a society.

The following information is vital to your understanding of Chapter 7. Explore it fully before you move on.

- The three cultural forces of social change:
  - Discovery: A new perception of an aspect of an already-known reality. When this new knowledge is acted on, it can induce social change.
  - Invention: A combination of existing and new knowledge to create something new. All inventions are dependent on past knowledge. Inventions can change society drastically.
  - Cultural diffusion: The spread of cultural elements from one society to another through trade, travel, migration, conquest, etc. These newly imported elements can cause changes in thoughts and processes and lead to social change.

- Three components of modernization:
  - Industrialization: A shift from human to non-human energy used during the manufacturing process.
  - Urbanization: Movement from rural to urban areas where manufacturing factories are located.
  - Bureaucratization: An increase in large, formal organizations.

- The five conditions of collective behavior:
  - Environmental factors: Timing and ease of communication add to the likelihood of spontaneous behavior.
  - Lack of norms: An absence of developed norms that will guide actions.
  - Conflicting values and norms: The existence of contradictory cultural elements.
  - Relative deprivation: The occurrence of people not having what they think they deserve.
  - Breakdown of social control: A failure of police to perform their roles or a loss of confidence in the system.

- Types of crowds:
  - Casual crowd: A loosely structured, usually passive group with little emotional interaction. Members enter and leave at will.
  - Conventional crowd: More structured with more predictable behavior. Members choose to be a part.
  - Expressive crowd: Structured around a celebration or event and allows expressive emotions.
  - Solidaristic crowds: Members have a strong sense of unity or agreement.
  - Acting crowds: An expressive crowd turned angry and hostile.

- Two types of acting crowds:
  1. Mobs: Threatens violence or is violent toward a single target.
  2. Riots: Violent and angry toward multiple, changing, targets and includes looting, property damage, and assault.

- Types of mass behavior:
  - Fashion: A temporarily popular style of dress or behavior that departs from what is customary.
  - Fad: A temporary fascination followed by a large number of people.
  - Craze: An intense fad that leaves lasting consequences and becomes part of the culture when it ends.
  - Panic: A collective behavior of those facing an incoming threat; fear, spontaneity, and lack of coordination are hallmarks of panic actions.
  - Mass hysteria: A widespread anxiety that is caused by an irrational belief and results in irrational behavior.
  - Disaster behavior: Following natural disasters, normal activities are disrupted and heterogeneous groups develop in the face of the chaotic aftermath.

- Types of mass communication:
  - Rumor: An unconfirmed piece of information passed from one person to another (and another and so on).
  - Gossip: Non-essential discussion of another's personal lives and actions.
  - Mass media: The strongest force shaping public opinion, these forms of media (newspaper, television, internet, and radio) aim to reach as much of the population as possible.
  - Urban legends: Realistic but untrue stories that often have a twist or irony concerning a recent event(s).

- Common types of social movements:
  - Reform movements: Seek to improve society; they are the most common and are generally accepted by society.
  - Revolutionary movements: Seek to overthrow or replace an existing social structure; they develop when participants are dissatisfied with the government's inattention or rejection.
    i. Few revolutionary movements have been successful; those that have been have brought great change and influenced societies across the globe.
  - Resistance (regressive) movements: Seek to reverse or resist change and revert society to more traditional values.
  - Expressive (utopian) movements: Seek to create "perfect societies" by separating from the larger society and establishing a community that promises to meet every

need.
- Millenarian (religious) movements: Seek to disrupt religious or spiritual practices.

Chapter Review

Activity 1: Matching
Match the fields of scientific study with the appropriate definition.

1. Sociology
2. Science
3. Natural Sciences
4. Social Sciences
5. Anthropology
6. Economics
7. Psychology
8. Social Psychology
9. Political Science
10. Political Sociology

A. Any logical, systematic method by which knowledge can be acquired; also the actual body of knowledge produced by such methods.
B. The study of human evolution and culture that focuses on small-scale, primitive societies.
C. The study of various aspects of human behavior.
D. The study of how personality and behavior are influenced by social elements.
E. A systematic approach to thinking about, studying, and understanding society, human social behavior, and social groups.
F. The study of physical and biological phenomena.
G. The study of production, distribution, and consumption of goods and services.
H. The study of social interaction involved in the process of government.
I. The study of mental processes and perception in individuals.
J. The study of political power, political processes, and governmental systems.

Activity 2: Matching
Match the different branches of anthropology to the appropriate definition.

1. Archaeology
2. Linguistics
3. Physical Anthropology
4. Cultural Anthropology
5. History
6. Human Ecology

A. Using fossils to trace human evolution.
B. The study of relationships between organisms and their environment.
C. Study of material remains from past cultures.
D. Study of causes and meanings of past events.
E. Study of pre-modern ways of life.
F. Study of human speech.

Activity 3: Multiple Choice
Identify the correct answer to the question.

1. Sociology is the study of:
   A. Society
   B. Human social behavior
   C. Social groups
   D. All of the above

2. Which of the following fields of study is not labeled a social science?
   A. Anthropology
   B. Psychology
   C. Chemistry
   D. Sociology

3. The listings of key terms should only be utilized at what stage of a study?
   A. Before
   B. During
   C. After
   D. Any of the above

4. Science is:
   A. Logical and systematic
   B. Illogical and messy
   C. Hard to understand
   D. Mastered by none

Activity 4: Short Answer
Answer the questions or prompts as fully as possible using the knowledge you have gained in this chapter.

1. What is the difference between physical anthropology and cultural anthropology?

2. What is the key difference between sociology and psychology?

3. What are the two main types of science and what are their differences and similarities?

Chapter Review Answers

Activity 1:
1. E
2. A
3. F
4. C
5. B
6. G
7. I
8. D
9. J
10. H

Activity 2:
1. C
2. F
3. A
4. E
5. D
6. B

Activity 3:
1. D
2. C
3. D
4. A

Activity 4:
1. The difference lies in what they each seek to find. Physical anthropology seeks to trace human evolution using fossils and other evidence. Cultural anthropology seeks to study the ways of life of pre-modern societies.
2. While psychology deals with the mental processes and behaviors of individuals, sociology deals with group behavior.
3. The two types of science are natural and social. Natural sciences study physical and biological phenomena. Social sciences study various aspects of human behavior. Natural sciences tend to be more objective, whereas social sciences tend to be more subjective. Even though they differ in these ways, they have a very important similarity: They both operate under the assumption that an underlying order exists in everything they study within the universe. This assumption allows them to observe, test, and make generalizations.

Chapter 2: The Sociological Perspective

What's the point?

- To review the definition of sociology.
- To understand the history of the field of sociology and the influence that exerts on today's sociological studies.
- To identify the earliest sociologists and uncover what they contributed to the field.
- To discover how sociological research is conducted.
- To understand the various sociological theories.

As the previous chapter stated, sociology is a relatively new field of scientific inquiry. Even though, it is a relative youngster in the academic line-up, there is still a plethora of information to be studied to gain a full understanding of the scope of the field. For instance, what is the origin of sociology? How did it come to be recognized as a legitimate field of study? Who were the founding figures? How have those beginnings evolved into the current set of theories that are used in studying group behaviors and society? These questions and many more will be answered in this chapter.

As Chapter 1 stated, sociology is a systematic approach to thinking about, studying, and understanding society, human social behavior, and social groups. Three things must be gleaned to begin to fully understand the science of sociology:

1. The history of the field
2. The historical and modern theories used
3. The methods used to research it

The History and Development of Sociology

Sociology has roots back into the 18th century European Enlightenment era, but it did not fully emerge until the social upheaval of the mid-19th century Industrial Revolution. The development of industry quickly changed the accepted social landscape. What was happening in society? Who could explain the changes and shifts?

Another key piece of kindling that started the sociological fire was the continued exposure of Europeans to the vastly different cultures of the Americas, Asia, and Africa. Why were these people's customs so different?

Founding Sociologists

Many key thinkers emerged during the Industrial Revolution who each shed light on this new area of thought by probing in new directions, enlightening previous theories, correcting flaws, clarifying terms and conditions. Here are a few notable names:

Auguste Comte:

A French philosopher by the name of Auguste Comte (1798-1857) is considered the founder of sociology. He coined the term "sociology" and proposed two initial areas of study in which the methods of science should be applied to studying society:

- Social statistics: The study of order and stability in society.
- Social dynamics: The study of a society's ability to adapt to changes, both internal and external.

Herbert Spencer:

Considered one of the greatest English social thinkers of his time, Herbert Spencer (1820-1903) applied Charles Darwin's theory of evolution to societies in order to explain social order and change and the problems that arise from those two areas. Treating societies as self-regulating organisms, he posited that societies evolved from simple to complex forms, just as Darwin theorized organisms had. Those organisms that adapt easily to their surroundings are more likely to thrive and reproduce – in animals and societies. Spencer, therefore, was an early advocate of Social Darwinism, or survival of the fittest society. He was against governmental interference in social affairs, claiming natural laws would be hindered – adversely affecting everyone.

Many of Spencer's theories have been discounted, but his analogous comparison of societies and organisms is now a staple within the modern functionalist theory.

Karl Marx:

One of the most influential men of the entire 19th century, Karl Marx (1818-1883), was influential in many scientific circles, such as philosophy, economics, political science, and history. His brilliant writings inspired modern Socialist and Communist movements.

Though Marx did not consider himself a sociologist, his insights are held in such high regard and have been so valuable, that he is now considered one of the most original and influential social thinkers. Marx insisted that a social scientist must not simply attempt to describe society, but he or she was to change it.

In Marx's view, societies were constantly in a state of conflict and revolution of which the key was class conflict, that is, the struggles between the "haves" and "have nots." The result of this conflict was a change in society. In this way, the economy has a fundamental influence on society.

Marx's conflict theories are widely accepted by modern sociologists.

Emile Durkheim:
The French sociologist Emile Durkheim (1858-1917) was a strong influence in the study of social order. He argued that societies are unified by shared values and beliefs, especially religious and ritual customs. Durkheim sought to discover the function of particular elements within a social system and how those functions contributed to the entire system and its maintenance.

Durkheim's social approach has greatly influenced modern American sociology.

Suicide: Sociological Reasons

Emile Durkheim made one of the first breakthroughs in sociological research with his study of suicides. By examining different population groups, he showed conclusively that suicide rates vary consistently from group to group, indicating that suicide is not simply an act of isolation, but that it is also influenced by society.

The four types of suicide are:
1. Egotistic: Victim does not feel connected to the larger society.
2. Altruistic: Victim places the welfare of others above own life.
3. Fatalistic: Victim feels powerless to regulate own life.
4. Anomic: Victim response to social disorder.

Max Weber:
Considered the most influential in western sociology, the German sociologist Max Weber (1864-1920) charged that not all social change is good. The industrial societies were moving in a negative direction and bureaucracy disenchanted everyone, or so Weber thought. On one hand, Weber welcomed the trend toward more equality, but also resisted, as he could foresee that the trend was leading to more governmental power of individuals.

Weber read, and admired, much of Marx's writings, but took issue with a few particulars.

- Where Marx said social change could always be traced to economy, Weber insisted that other factors such as religious ideas could be instigators of social change.
- Where Marx viewed value judgments (opinions based on personal values) to be acceptable, Weber insisted that value judgments have no place in the professional work of sociologists.
- Where Marx viewed social change as a mostly positive occurrence, Weber argued that it can sometimes lead to negative, not positive, outcomes. (See above).
-

Modern Developments

The United States has been the predominant canvas for the modern development of sociology. The rise of urban issues led American sociologists to research the problem in the hopes of finding a legitimate means of housing reform.

In 1892, the University of Chicago was the first educational institution to offer a doctoral degree in Sociology. Called the "Chicago School," the researchers assembling there studied immigration, urbanization, and racial relations. Within twenty years, the study of sociology became a widely known discipline.

The leading members of the Chicago School were:

George Herbert Mead	The study of how individuals fit into, interact with, and alter the roles in a social system.
Robert Park	Leading member.
Lester Ward	Focused on social progress guided by sociological knowledge.
Talcott Parsons	Viewed society as a stable but complex system of interdependent parts, each performing important functions in a system.
Robert Merton	Known for "middle-range theories," an approach that aimed at integrating theory with empirical research.
Peter Berger	Developed "debunking," or looking below the surface of social experiences.
C. Wright Mills	Challenged Parsons' view. Established theories about the power elite which led to research on the American power structure.

Table 1: Leading Members of Chicago School

Today's sociologists are not bound to study in one particular area of sociological perspective. Their professional roles are diverse (to be discussed in a later chapter) and the field of sociology is a well-established, legitimate discipline. Today's sociologists are still deciding whether Weber's value-free approach or Marx's activist approach is correct, and perhaps both are depending on the situation.

Whichever stance they take and whichever societal development they research, modern sociologists are still using the basis of many of the theories put forth by the originators of the field.

Sociological Theory

A key component of the sciences is theory – an organized statement that lays out a set of concepts in a significantly relevant way in order to explain the relationship among them. If a theory is found to be valid, predictions about identical relationships can be made based on the known theory. Theories are important to scientific study because a solid theory allows the facts of research to be understandable; it allows events to be placed in a meaningful framework to identify cause and effect, to explain, or to predict.

In sociology, theories vary widely because of the vast differences in the assumptions that each sociologists holds. Broad assumptions about society and social behavior that provides a point of view for the study of specific problems, a _theoretical perspective_, guide the formation of most sociological theories. Modern sociology makes use of three general theoretical perspectives: functionalist, conflict, and interactionist points of view. Each perspective is based on certain assumptions and leads to different conclusions in the analysis of society.

Functionalist Point of View:
Originating with the thoughts of Spencer and Durkheim, the _functionalist perspective_ views society as a whole consisting of various parts, each of which have different functions necessary for the stability of the whole; it also focuses on why societies assume the particular forms that they each do. As noted previously, Spencer compared societies to living organisms in terms of structure and function; he posited that societies have structure, or sets of interrelated parts that contribute to the overall stability of the structure.

The functionalist perspective was refined by Talcott Parsons and Robert Merton, Parsons' student, in more modern times as they, among other functionalist theorists, insisted that society tends to be organized and stable (when most members of the society are in agreement on the same set of basic beliefs) because of the inter-relationship between its parts. This stability is known as equilibrium, or balance. Social change is considered negative unless it is a slow moving change. Small changes in one portion of the system instigate small changes in other parts of the system, thus leading to small changes throughout the social organism. Rapid change, however, in one portion tends to leave other parts unable to catch up and disequilibria results.

Robert Merton defined two terms used when distinguishing what is the function of a particular element of a social system. First, to define a function, sociologists identify what the consequence of the action is, rather than what the purposes are believed to be. A _manifest function_ is an obvious consequence, and a _latent function_ is an unintended consequence. Merton also differentiated negative consequences.

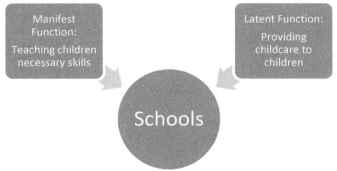

Figure 1: Example of Manifest and Latent Functions

Such dysfunctions could disrupt the social balance. It is possible that a function could be both functional and dysfunctional simultaneously.

Some sociological theorists criticize the functionalist viewpoint as being too conservative. They claim that the emphasis on order and stability forces functionalists to dismiss negative consequences as dysfunctional even if those particular functions are necessary or inevitable, or in the long run (but not immediately) beneficial.

The functionalist perspective is sometimes referred to as order perspective, structural functionalism, or systems theory.

Conflict Point of View:

Originating from Karl Marx, the conflict perspective focuses on the struggles resulting from tension, competition, and change in society. Marx viewed class struggles as the primary source of conflict and change in society. On the whole, this theory was not accepted in American sociological circles until the 1960s.

C. Wright Mills, Ralf Dahrendorf, and Randall Collins refined the conflict point of view. They shied away from prioritizing class conflict as Marx did. They branched out and saw conflicts in many different groups and categories of society. It is this modern definition that encompasses many people groups and stratifications that persists today.

According to these sociological theorists, societies are constantly changing; conflict is a given. The conflict perspective is completely at odds with the functionalist point of view because it states that society is in a constant state of conflict. This conflict is not always considered a negative thing; it is often beneficial and instigates positive change.

Conflict theorists view the form of society as the product of the most powerful individuals who coerce the rest of the population into their view of what the society should look like. Social order only exists by force or the threat of it. For example, large groups of workers can unite and cause a disturbing turn-out at a picket or rally. Their conflict can engender improvements in working conditions.

Interactionist Point of View:

Max Weber introduced interactionist perspective, which is a consideration of how the parts of a society act and react. George Herbert Mead later refined the theory. The interactionist viewpoint considers the smaller interactions between people; it does not look at the overall structure of a society like the functionalist theory does, nor does it look at the setup of class structures as the conflict theory does. The backbone of the interactionist perspective is the thought that it is individuals who are always in the process of developing their society.

One type of interaction that is common to everyone is symbolic interaction. It is the interaction with items of symbolic value in the society. For example, obeying traffic signals or following the advice of a newspaper article. A symbol is anything that represents something else.
There are many viewpoints that reside within the boundaries of the interactionist perspective. Some of them are as follows:

Viewpoint	Related Sociologists	Description
Dramaturgical Approach	Erving Goffman	Life is viewed as a theater where everyone acts out their perceived roles and create their characters based on the reactions of others.
Exchange Approach	George Homans	Behavior is influenced by punishments and rewards. The world consists of people interacting and mutually rewarding or punishing each other.
Looking Glass Self	Charles Horton Cooley	A person views themselves based on the reactions of others.
Self-Fulfilling Prophecy		A certain predicament is expected. Behavior then follows that expectation. The reaction to that behavior qualifies the original prediction.

Table 2: Common Interactionist Viewpoints

How individuals react to others is largely dependent on how they perceive the other person's message. How they perceive the message is largely dependent on their past experiences in similar situations.

A Note on Objectivity in Sociology:
Sociologists cannot free themselves from bias completely. After all, sociology is a study of humans carried out by humans, naturally subjective beings. Subjectivity is implemented when a decision is made on the basis of a person's values or experiences. Objectivity is implemented when a decision is made on the basis of mathematical data or other non-personal information. The primary means of combating bias in the social sciences is to present sociological findings to others; an open forum for discussion and criticism can help sociologists remain objective.

Research Methods
There are two types of sociology and the differences between these two approaches are best understood by examining the different research methods used in each.

- Applied (direct) sociology: Uses research to find solutions to practical problems.

- <u>Academic (indirect) sociology:</u> Uses research to discover knowledge, simply for the sake of obtaining knowledge.

Generally, sociological research happens outside the confines of a lecture room – in the real world. To produce reliable studies, it is imperative that sociologists develop a <u>methodology</u>, the set of standards and procedures that will guide their experimentation or observation. A proper methodology allows the findings of the procedure to be duplicated and researched by other sociologists by providing guidelines for evidence collection. Questions must have observable and verifiable factual answers.

Scientific inquiry insists that every event has a cause; under the right circumstances, that cause will always result in the same effect. There are two types of <u>empirical research</u>, research that uses direct observation through sight and sound:

- <u>Descriptive studies:</u> Explain what is happening and why.
- <u>Explanatory studies:</u> Explain how things are happening and why.

Sociologists examine a plethora of cause and effect relationships. When enough of the same type of observation is present, they can make a generalization, or label a sociological concept, which can be either tangible or intangible. These concepts are often variables in the research being done. A variable is a characteristic that is subject to change. For example, age can be a variable. When one variable is seen to have an influence on another variable, causation has been found. The two types of variables that exist are:

- <u>Independent variable:</u> The variable that does the influencing.
- <u>Dependent variable:</u> The variable that is influenced.

Generally, sociologists have an idea of what is going to happen. They use generalizations, or statements of likelihood, not certainty, to hypothesize. To actually determine if a cause and effect relationship exists, a sociologist must establish that a correlation exists between the studied behaviors. To determine whether a causal relationship exists, sociologists will also use controls to eliminate any other possible reasons for the observed results.

Qualitative vs. Quantitative:
Applied research methods are either qualitative or quantitative in nature. <u>Quantitative methods</u> use measurable quantities; numbers and statistics are common elements of a quantitative study. <u>Qualitative methods</u> use a verbal form of description. The strengths and weaknesses of each method are continually debated in scientific circles. Researchers often decide on which method to use based on their own personality or thinking style along with their culture or organization of origin.

The following table illustrates the main differences between the two methodologies.

Distinguishing Features of Qualitative and Quantitative Research	
Qualitative	Quantitative
Goal: Complete, detailed description.	Goal: Order features, count specifics, create models – all in an effort to explain observations.
Advance knowledge: Researcher has only a rough estimate or hypothesis of what to look for.	Advance knowledge: Researcher clearly knows what data he/she is looking for.
Design: Continually developed throughout the study.	Design: Carefully developed before any data collection is done.
Data gathering instrument: The researcher	Data gathering instrument: Tools, equipment, questionnaire, etc.
Data: Words, pictures, objects	Data: Numbers, statistics
Subjective	Objective
Time consuming	Efficient
Generalization is harder	Generalizations may be easier
Researcher can become immersed or intermingled with subject matter.	Researcher usually becomes separated from subject matter.

Table 3: Differences of Qualitative and Quantitative Methodologies

While the differences are often highlighted and debated, it is important to realize that the two methods can be integrated. Such integrated studies often lead to far more advanced understanding than either single approach.

In general, there are five methods sociologists used in their research: social experiments, surveys, observational studies, case studies, and research evaluation.

Social Experiments:
In a <u>social experiment</u>, two variables are observed and the relationship between them is determined in carefully controlled environments. When in a laboratory, the researcher obviously has more control than when he or she is experimenting in the field. When in the field, though, more natural results are possible.

The <u>independent variable</u> is the variable that is changed or used at different levels in an effort to elicit a change in the dependent variable. The environment of a social experiment is carefully designed and controlled to ensure that the independent variable is the only possible reason for any difference in outcomes. The <u>dependent variable</u> is the variable that is likely to change when the independent variable is altered. The <u>experimental group</u> is the group that is exposed to the independent variable. The <u>control group</u> is the group that is not.
The <u>Hawthorne effect</u> occurs when an individual's assumptions about an experiment affect that individual's results – either positively or negatively.

Advantages	Disadvantages
Valuable research techniques that allows for the study of a variety of experimental topics.	In an artificial environment, subject can act differently than they would in the same situation in a natural environment.
Can easily determine casual relationships.	The method is only usable in clearly defined cases.
	Researcher contamination is common.

Table 4: Advantages and Disadvantages of Social Experiments

Surveys:

A survey is a systematic and standardized means of collecting data. Surveys are utilized because of their efficiency in collecting facts and the relationship between certain facts. Because of time and financial constraint, a sample (usually random) of the population, not the entire population, is asked to respond.

In order to conduct a survey, a questionnaire or an interview must be developed, or a combination of the two forms. The questionnaire technique is based on a standard form that respondents fill out and return. The interview technique is used when a researcher asks the respondents questions. The interview can be either:

- Structured: Inflexible; each subject asked the exact same questions in the exact same order and he or she chooses the best of the predetermined possible answers.
- Unstructured: Subjects are asked open-ended questions.

The following table covers some of the advantages and disadvantages of using surveys for sociological research.

Advantages	Disadvantages
Efficient way to gather information	Only usable in certain situations with certain topics
Unstructured: Allows for greater insight	Unstructured: Responses are harder to analyze
	Researcher has to be extra careful in word choice and facial expression

Table 5: Advantages and Disadvantages of Surveys

Observational Studies:

Observational studies, describing real-time observations of naturally-occurring events, are commonly used in sociological research. When performing this type of research, it is of the utmost importance to strictly record observations, not interpretations of those observations. When a researcher stays out of the action, he or she is conducting nonparticipant observations. If the researcher becomes personally involved in what is happening, he or she is involved with a participant observation.

The table below contrasts the advantages and disadvantages of observational studies.

Advantages	Disadvantages
Natural environment is conducive to natural actions and reactions	Only usable in certain situations with certain topics
Can observe common behaviors within a small group	Cannot determine causal relationships

Table 6: Advantages and Disadvantages of Observational Studies

Case Study:

The most common type of field observation, the case study provides a detailed record of an event, either past or present, a group, or a social process. When studying a past event, the researcher pieces together as complete a picture as possible using interviews, news articles, and public records.

Advantages	Disadvantages
Reveals tremendous insights	Sacrifices precision
Large amount of data available	

Table 7: Advantages and Disadvantages of Case Studies

Research Evaluation:

Sometimes, researchers use already-available information. This is known as research evaluation. Public information is available from several places, like the Census Bureau. A wealth of information is also available from other sociologists. This already-in-existence data is quicker than creating new experiments, but it is also subject to trusting others for accurate information.

Other Research Methods:

Here is a listing of other, lesser-used, methods of sociological experimentation.

Approach	Explanation
Comparative Analysis	Comparing multiple systems from different points of time.
Replication	Repeating a study to verify accuracy.
Unobtrusive Measures	Keeping out of the way of subjects; not imposing self on subjects.
Community Studies	Lot of information is collected about a small area to provide enough detail to understand the community.

Table 8: Description of Other Research Methods

Sociological Research Method

Like all scientific research, sociological studies follow a basic step-by-step process. The ideal model is listed below; it is important to realize that the model is a guideline, not a list of necessary steps. Some details can be overlooked if it is for the betterment (or increased accuracy of) your experiment, but overall these are the steps to take when designing your experiment or observation.

- Define problem→Pick a topic
- Review known information→Previous findings by other researchers→What questions still need to be answered?
- Hypothesize→Predict relationship between tested variables→State purpose of research in measurable terms
- Design research process→What information is to be collected?→How is the data to be analyzed?
- Gather data→Record information
- Analyze data→Classify facts→Make correlations; generalize outcomes
- Draw conclusion→Provide detailed write-up of results

Figure 2: Sociological Research Model

Research Difficulties:
Sociology involves humans. Because it involves humans, there is a level of complexity that is expected in any experimentation. There are a number of specific challenges that arise during the study of humans.

For example:

- Subjects are aware that they are being studied.
- Subjects can alter their behavior to suit their mood, not the variables.
- Subjects may give false information to make themselves seem better.
- Cause and effect relationships are hard to accurately decipher because of the complexities of human behavior.

Another area that poses difficulty is researcher attachment. If the subject matter is emotionally significant for the researcher, it may be difficult for the researcher to resist distorting the findings to their preconceived expectations.

Max Weber used subjective interpretation, called Verstehen, the understanding of human activities, to attempt to decipher correlations between variables. He felt that sociologists should try and put themselves into the shoes of their subjects (figuratively, not literally).

Ethical Issues:

Certain ethical issues arise, like the right to privacy, and can cause issues in sociological experiments. Some individuals may feel it is an invasion of privacy for a person to observe them without telling them they are doing so. For example, a participant observer who disguises himself as part of the group – not a researcher – may be cornered by questions of privacy.

While it may be obvious that experimenters should not harm patients, it is a viable concern, as it has occurred in the past. Because of these usually unintended harmful consequences, informed consents are commonly used in sociological experimentation today. Informed consents are detailed explanations of what will be going on in the experiment; the subject is to sign the consent before being a part of the study. The downside to this is that the chances of the Hawthorne effect showing up are greatly increased.

The very nature of sociological research can be used in a multitude of arenas. When the researcher shares some sort of relationship with the funding institution, it may unduly pressure the researcher to skew the findings toward a preferred outcome.

Even with the ethical issues involved in sociological research, there are great gains in the understanding of human behaviors and decision-making through appropriate and professional research.

Terms to Remember:

Term	Definition
Population	The tested or observed group of people.
Population Sample	Representative selection of the entire population.
Respondents	Tested individuals; subjects.
Random Sample	Selection of test subjects chosen in a random manner.

Chapter Review

Activity 1: Matching
Match the early sociologist with the appropriate development or field of study.

1. Auguste Comte
2. Herbert Spencer
3. Karl Marx
4. Emile Durkheim
5. Max Weber
6. Robert Park
7. Lester Ward
8. George Herbert Mead
9. Talcott Parsons
10. Robert Merton
11. Peter Berger
12. C. Wright Mills

A. French sociologist who insisted societies are unified by shared beliefs and values.
B. Englishman who applied Darwin's theory of evolution to societies.
C. French founder of sociology. Coined the term 'sociology.'
D. German sociologist most influential in western sociology.
E. German who believed that societies are always in a state of conflict and resolution.
F. Developed "debunking or looking below the surface of social experiences.
G. Viewed society as a stable but complex system of interdependent parts, each performing important functions in a system.
H. Leading member of the Chicago School.
I. Known for 'middle-range theories' as an approach that aimed at integrating theory with empirical research.
J. Established theories about the power elite which led to research on the American power structure.
K. Developed social psychology.
L. Focused on social progress guided by sociological knowledge.

Activity 2: Matching
Match the type of suicide as elaborated by Durkheim with the appropriate definition.

1. Egotistic
2. Altruistic
3. Fatalistic
4. Anomic

A. Victim responds to social disorder.
B. Victim has feelings of powerless to regulate.
C. Victim feels disconnected from society.
D. Victim places the welfare of others above self.

Activity 3: Matching

Match the terms to the appropriate definition.

1. Chicago School
2. Theory
3. Theoretical Perspective
4. Manifest Function
5. Latent Function
6. Symbolic Interactions
7. Symbol
8. Subjectivity
9. Objectivity
10. Methodology
11. Social Concept
12. Variable
13. Causation
14. Population
15. Population Sample
16. Random Sample
17. Respondents
18. Qualitative Method
19. Quantitative Method

A. Broad assumptions about society and social behavior that provides a point of view for the study of specific problems.
B. A selection of test subjects that is representative of the entire population.
C. The first educational institution offering a doctoral degree in sociology.
D. Anything that represents something else.
E. Basing a decision on one's own feelings or experiences.
F. The tested individuals; test subjects.
G. When one variable is found to influence another.
H. Unintended consequence.
I. A characteristic that is subject to change.
J. The tested or observed group of people.
K. Obvious consequence.
L. A generalization discovered by observation.
M. The set of standards and procedure that guide a sociologist's experimentation or observation.
N. Selection of test subjects chosen in a random manner.
O. Interacting with items of symbolic value in society.
P. A type of research procedure that uses measurable quantities; numbers and statistics are common.
Q. An organized statement that lays out a set of concepts in a significantly relevant way in order to explain the relationship among them.
R. Basing a decision on factual information, like mathematical data.
S. A type of research procedure that uses a more description verbal approach to collecting data.

Activity 4: Matching
Match the different psychological theory to the appropriate definition.

1. Social Statistics
2. Social Dynamics
3. Social Darwinism
4. Social Psychology
5. Functional Perspective
6. Conflict Perspective
7. Interactionist Perspective
8. Academic Sociology
9. Applied Sociology

A. Survival of the fittest society.
B. Focuses on the struggles resulting from tension, competition, and change in societies.
C. The study of how an individual fits into, interacts with, and alters the roles in a social system.
D. Sociological research that researchers to increase knowledge.
E. Study of order and stability.
F. Study of society's ability to adapt to change, both internal and external.
G. Sociological research that strives to find answers to immediate and practical problems.
H. The consideration of how parts of a society act and react.
I. Views society as a whole consisting of various parts, each of which has different functions necessary for the stability of the whole; and it focuses on why societies assume the particular forms that they each do.

Activity   5:   Matching
Match the research method with the appropriate definition.

1. Social Experiment
2. Surveys
3. Observational Study
4. Case Study
5. Research Evaluation

A. Systematic (and usually standardized) way of collecting data.
B. Simple method of research that involves describing live events that are occurring in a natural environment.
C. Making use of information already in existence.
D. An applied research technique that involves determining the relationship between two variables while the variables are in a carefully controlled environment.
E. The most detailed accounts of an event, group, or social process – past or present.

Activity 6: Matching
Match the terms to the appropriate definition.

1. Independent Variable
2. Dependent Variable
3. Experimental Group
4. Control Group
5. Hawthorne Effect

A. The group under the influence of the independent variable.
B. When the knowledge of an experiment taints the results.
C. The variable that is used at different levels in an attempt to elicit a change in the dependent variable.
D. The group that is not influenced by the independent variable.
E. Variable that is less likely to change when the independent variable changes.

Activity 7: Multiple Choice
Select the most appropriate response for each question.

1. The conflict perspective:
    A. States that conflict is an inevitable part of society
    B. Is associated with Karl Marx and Ralf Dahrendorf
    C. Primarily focuses on social change as it occurs through conflict
    D. All of the above

2. Which prominent sociologist states the bureaucracies were disenchanting societies?
    A. Max Weber
    B. Herbert Spencer
    C. Karl Marx
    D. Emile Durkheim

3. Which sociologist gravitated toward the dramaturgical approach?
    A. Erving Goffman
    B. George Herbert Mead
    C. Max Weber
    D. Karl Marx

4. Generalizations are:
    A. Correlations
    B. Statements of probability
    C. Gender specific
    D. Methods of research

5. Surveys
    A. Are gender specific
    B. Are carefully constructed
    C. Can evaluate a population's attitude toward something
    D. Are not systematic

6. When a correlation exists between two variables,
    A. A meaningful relationship exists between the two variables
    B. There is no relationship at all
    C. Causation is assumed not exist

7. Karl Marx is associated with conflict theory.
    A. True
    B. False

8. Which group in a sociological experiment is not exposed to the independent variable?
    A. Research group
    B. Control group
    C. Experimental group
    D. Sample group

Activity 8: Short Answer

Answer the questions or prompts as fully as possible using the knowledge you have gained in this chapter.

1. What are the three main perspectives in sociological study?

2. What is the primary difference between objectivity and subjectivity?

3. Define independent and dependent variables.

4. Outline the sociological research model.

Chapter Review Answers

Activity 1:
1. C
2. B
3. E
4. A
5. D
6. H
7. L
8. K
9. G
10. I
11. F
12. J

Activity 2:
1. C
2. D
3. B
4. A

Activity 3:
1. C
2. Q
3. A
4. K
5. H
6. O
7. D
8. E
9. R
10. M
11. L
12. I
13. G
14. J
15. B
16. N

17. F
18. S
19. P

Activity 4:
1. E
2. F
3. A
4. C
5. I
6. B
7. H
8. D
9. G

Activity 5:
1. D
2. A
3. B
4. E
5. C

Activity 6:
1. C
2. E
3. A
4. D
5. B

Activity 7:
1. D
2. A
3. A
4. B
5. C
6. D
7. A

8. B

Activity 8:
1. Functionalist, Conflict, and Interactionist Perspectives.
2. The primary difference is the factors related to the decision. Objective decisions are based on facts, whereas subjective decisions are based on ideas, feelings, or values.
3. The independent variable is the variable that is being introduced or purposefully changed as the experiment proceeds. The dependent variable is what changes as the independent variable does.
4. Define problem – Review Known Information – Hypothesize – Design Research Process – Gather Data – Analyze Data – Draw Conclusions

Chapter 3: Social Processes, Part 1

> **What's the point?**
>
> - To define relevant terms in the culture, social interaction, and socialization realms of sociology.
> - To understand what 'culture' is and how it affects sociological studies.
> - To explain theories of social interaction.
> - To familiarize students with important theorists and theories of socialization.

Culture

Sociologists consider <u>culture</u> to be all the shared material and nonmaterial products of a society, the system developed to define a way of life for a society or group. Specifically, <u>material culture</u> is made up of physical objects created and valued by members of a society, like buildings, businesses, clothing, automobiles, factories, etc. <u>Nonmaterial culture</u> revolves around abstract, intangible human creations, including rules, knowledge, values, politics, language, myths, beliefs, etc.

Culture and society are two completely different entities. While culture is the product of an interactive society, <u>society</u> is made up of people who share a culture. The two terms are interrelated and dependent on each other. Without one, the other cannot exist.

Culture is not only shared across generations, but it is dependent on each subsequent generation learning it. Along with their biological disposition, the culture an individual learns and grows in greatly influences their behavior. Rather than the instincts of animals, most researchers refer to simple reflexes and basic drives when discussing humanity's common behaviors. <u>Simple reflexes</u> are involuntary muscle responses. <u>Basic drives</u> are urges for the fulfillment of basic needs, like self-preservation, food, drink, and sex. Culture helps to dictate just how a person goes about fulfilling these drives; culture establishes what is acceptable and what is not.

Cultural Components

Culture is constrained by several factors. <u>Norms</u> control the behavior of a society; they act as a set of guidelines that establish what is accepted as appropriate behavior in given situations. Social life flows smoother when guidelines like this are adopted. Some norms apply to society in general, while others only apply to certain groups or certain situations. For the most part, all members of a society readily conform to the established norms. The three social norms are folkways, mores, and law.

- Folkways cover the ordinary and everyday conventions of normal life. Nonconformity of a folkway is not considered immoral and is generally not illegal. An example of a folkway is making appointments and keeping them. A nonconformist would be one who breaks an appointment without calling. A nonconformist in this case is not labeled a pariah.
- Mores (pronounced "more-ays") are stronger and more significant morally. The nonconformity to a more is a more serious matter. In some cases, the breaking of it is repugnant to the general populace. For example, eating human flesh is revolting to most North Americans. Occasionally, it is hard to distinguish whether a cultural belief is a folkway or a more. It is possible that over time, the significance of something changes from a more serious more into a folkway – a preferred, but not mandated way of life.
- A law is a standard that is formally enacted by the political authority of a community. The power of the state is behind a law. Specific punishments are outlined for violators of laws. Every member of the community is expected to know and follow the list of codified laws. Often, laws are enacted to support strongly held norms of a society. Sometimes, laws change the norms, like the Civil Rights legislation of the 1960s did.

Generally, each society has some type of social control that enables the ruling authority to ensure that the population is following the laws. Conformity of all norms – codified or not – is rewarded by positive sanctions; nonconformity is punished by negative sanctions. (Sanctions will be discussed more in a later chapter).

Societies also share values, shared ideas of what is good, right, and desirable. While norms are specific and concrete, values are abstract in nature. Values influence a society's norms. American values are freedom, success, achievement, individualism, and progress. Different cultures value different ideals and solve problems in different ways.

> **The Arts**
> Along with norms, the artistic output of a culture is unique. Across the globe, there are a multitude of forms of artistic expression, each complimenting and reflecting the native culture of the artist.

Norms and values are often associated with a symbol, an agreed upon representation of something else. For example, the nation is represented by its flag. Freedom is represented by the eagle. Language is arguably the most important symbol of any culture. The written and spoken forms of human speech are essential to a society's health and well-being. Language permits the continuation of a culture. Without language, history and knowledge are lost.

Sociological Perspectives on Culture
Sociologists each view culture through a different lens, depending on which perspective they typically use in their sociological studies.

- *Functionalist Perspective:*
  Functionalists view society and culture as an organism with interdependent parts; each part meets some specific need of the entire community. Functionalists realize that some parts may be missing in some cultures, creating unique cultures with unique components. The one downfall to this perspective is the likelihood that cultural changes are often overlooked.

- *Conflict Perspective:*
  Conflict theorists view society as in a constant state of conflict, generally caused by competition and struggle between groups.

  Ideologies, cultural beliefs that justify one group's goals, are at the root of such conflict. Cultural change, according to the conflict perspective, occurs when different groups within a society rise to power or fall from it. When a new group rises to power, their norms become the norms and values of the whole.

- *Ecological Perspective:*
  Ecology is the study of the relationship between various organisms and their environments. Cultural ecology states that culture is formed by the limitations or excess of resources and other changes in the environment. Cultural ecologists insist that climate, geography, plant life, and animal life shape the cultures of the world. This is truer in simpler societies.

Universal Aspects across Cultures

Some aspects of different cultures are actually alike from society to society. There are a vast number of <u>universals</u>, or characteristics shared by many cultures. The figure at the right shows some of the most common. These practices are general; each culture creates their own form and expression of each. For example, marriage and family systems are present in every culture, but the structure varies widely.

Figure 3: Examples of Cultural Universals

Another universal aspect is <u>ethnocentrism</u>, the belief that one's own culture is the 'right' or 'normal' one. This is especially evident amongst isolated communities. While this is a type of patriotism, it can actually lead to racism and hostilities. Because of the way humans learn, most people tend to evaluate another culture by the standards of their own; this is known as <u>ethnocentric</u> thinking.

The antithesis of this thinking pattern is <u>cultural relativism</u>, the idea that another culture cannot be judged by the standards of one's own. This idea is necessary for sociologists; they will not be able to fully understand another culture unless they attempt to understand it within its own contexts.

Cultural Variations

Not only do differences exist between cultures, but differences are evident amongst groups within one culture. The differences are usually due to the disparity between the <u>ideal culture</u> (the established standard of norms and values) and the <u>real culture</u> (the actual norms and values practiced within a society). A man who states his belief in the sanctity of marriage is obviously disparaging his own belief when he sleeps with a woman who is not his wife. Groups that are part of the culture, but not completely interwoven with them create another source of variation. These <u>subcultures</u> tend to have their own subset of norms, values, and lifestyles. Subcultures develop across many platforms; they can be occupation related, race related, or age related, and they exist in every major modern society. A <u>counterculture</u>, on the other hand, has values, norms, and lifestyles completely at odds with that of the dominant culture. This is not always a negative (like the KKK), but can be positive (like the Amish).

Overall, <u>cultural integration</u>, the tendency toward certain mores, values, and beliefs even among the diverse groups of a society, must remain or the entire culture is open for extinction. Too rapid a change leads to dangerous territory for any society.

Because people are resistant to change, it usually occurs slowly. Cultural changes most often revolve around economic or environmental concerns. The three processes that lead to this kind of change are discovery, invention, and diffusion.

- <u>Discovery</u> is an increase in knowledge or insight.
- <u>Invention</u> is the new use of existing knowledge to create something that did not exist before.
- <u>Diffusion</u> is the spread of cultural elements from one culture into another.

Societal Structure

A <u>society</u> is a population that resides in the same physical territory, is under the authority of the same political entity, and shares the same common culture. Sociologists believe humans cannot survive without society. Many sociologists affirm that every human function is in some way 'social.'

Understanding the structure of societies leads to greater insights for researchers. <u>Social structure</u> is the pattern of interacting relationships among the different components of the society. In essence, social structure relates how the elements in a society relate to one another. Most social structures remain stable and offer a sense of security to the society. The efficiency of the structure, however, can leave little to no room for personal freedoms in regime-like societies.

A society's structure is comprised of: status, roles, groups, and institutions.

- <u>Status</u> is a person's position in a society. (A <u>social class</u> is a group of people in one society who have the same status.) An individual's status clearly defines his or her place in society and how he or she should relate to others. An individual can have many statuses at once. A <u>master status</u> is a person's most significant, or the one that identifies their social position the clearest. Often, an occupational status is the most dominant, usually because individuals spend so much of their time working. An <u>ascribed status</u> is one that a person has no control over, like race or gender. An <u>achieved status</u> is one that a person has earned; this type of status changes according to an individual's behaviors. On occasion, a <u>status inconsistency</u>, a contradictory set of statuses applied to one person, appears in a society.
- A <u>role</u> is an established pattern of behavior, usually associated with a set of obligations and privileges. Many roles are attached to a particular social status. In fact, a single status may have a <u>role set</u>, many related roles. Roles are more flexible and undergo redefinition almost constantly. <u>Role expectations</u> are the social norms attributed to a certain role and determine how a person behaves in that role. This may, in fact, contradict the actual <u>role performance</u>, or actual behavior exhibited by someone in that role. Sometimes, a person who has several different social statuses, each with different roles attached to it, can

become confused and experience <u>role confusion</u>. <u>Role strain</u> refers to the problem that results from too many expectations being inherent in one role. <u>Role conflict</u> is the problem that occurs when two or more of a person's roles contradict each other.

- A <u>group</u> is two or more people who share common ideas, feelings, or pursuits and who interact with a social structure. Most social interaction occurs in groups, also called social systems. A <u>primary group</u> is the smaller number of individuals who know one another and interact more frequently and intimately. A <u>secondary group</u> consists of persons in the same roles united in a specific, short-term, impersonal scenario.
    - An <u>aggregate</u> is different because it is made up of people who happen to be in the same location at the same time. <u>Social categories</u> are not technically groups, either, because they are people who are connected by an ideal, but who lack social structure.
- A <u>social institution</u> is an established set of roles, statuses, and groups, all of which share common norms and values that has developed out of social need. The common features of a social institution are:
    - Resistant to change
    - Unanimously accepted – usually without question
    - Interdependent
    - Successive change – when one institution changes, others tend to change as well
    - Failure of an institution equates to social problems

These structures of society are seen in communities throughout the nation; communities tend to focus on home and workplace structures and the daily interactions that occur there. A society is known as the cumulative institutions that are needed to meet the needs of humanity. The world system is an interrelated conjunction of all the societies in the world, interacting on economic, political, and cultural levels.

Perspectives on Societal Structure
The functionalist and conflict viewpoints each view the structure and makeup of society differently.

- *Functional Perspective:*
  Functionalists are concerned with the stability of the entire social system and how an institution affects that stability. Failure of an institution is labeled as a dysfunction and researchers with this perspective seek out how to repair the institution and return the system to greater stability.

- *Conflict Perspective:*
  Conflict theorists attempt to identify who is the benefactor to the existing social structure. They view institutional failure as the result of the ever present struggle between two or more groups seeking power or advantage.

Types of Societies

In general, societies grow from simple and small to larger and more complex. That's not to say that all societies grow exactly the same; that is not true. Some seem to grow overnight; others stagnate and seemingly remain the same; and still others have disappeared.

The ecological approach analyzes the entire environment as it correlates to society and culture. The five basic types of society are classified by the type of technology used to gather food and produce goods.

- *Hunting and Gathering Societies:*
  These small societies, often less than forty members, rely on catching wild animals and foraging native vegetation. Every society started as hunting and gathering societies that wandered from place to place as their food sources ran out. Contact with other societies was limited. Within these societies, few statuses existed and few to no specialized roles existed either. There was usually some differentiation between the young and old and men and women. The members of each society shared almost identical values. They tended not to accumulate wealth, but instead shared everything in an effort to meet their simple needs. Overall, they spend less time working than other societies.

- *Pastoral Societies:*
  In these growing societies, families rely on domesticated herd animals. They are more productive and reliable than hunting and gathering societies. Even though these societies often wander, seeking new and better grazing land, they are often larger because they can support a larger group of people. Trading offers the opportunity to acquire power as weapons and wealth is accumulated. Power and wealth always lead to more variety in status. Political and economic institutions grow and culture becomes more complex. Trade also opens the door for inter-society conflict. Slavery is sometimes seen as a result of these fights. In general, many of these societies believe in gods that tend to their needs.

- *Horticultural Societies:*
  These societies rely on the cultivation of domestic plants. Working by hand with hand tools, they remain settled in one area, only moving short distances as needed. These societies are more efficient than hunting and gathering. When able to store surpluses, power grows. As power grows, political institutions emerge forming new roles and class structures. As people become stationary (in a migration context), they put more time and effort into their artifacts, making them more elaborate.

- *Agrarian Societies:*
  Theses societies are an evolved version of the horticultural society. They rely on the cultivation of crops using tools, such as plows, and animal power. The plow was responsible for increasing food production and increasing agricultural output. Agrarian societies are much larger than horticultural and pastoral. The population can be as high as several million people. With the greater number of citizens, roles outside of farming develop; culture becomes even more complex, and new social classes and roles become available. Cities are established, and

government entities emerge, including a concentrate power, like a monarchy. Wealth becomes unequally shared which spurs trade. The greater role of trade encourages the development of currency; it also provides another reason for the development of written language (along with government regulations and taxation). Religion becomes a separate entity or institution, and military organizations evolve as war erupts between societies.

- *Industrialized Societies:*
  These societies rely on mechanized production facilities instead of animal or human power. This type of society is rapidly emerging as a dominant force in today's world. Technological changes are constantly being developed, leaving these societies in a constant state of change. Improved standards of living increase the possible population limits, which becomes highly urban.

  Government and bureaucracies thrive in the large industrial population. Because of the more technical job force, education is a more necessary part of life. The inequalities inherent in social class structure are more easily overcome, and representative governments evolve to voice the opinions of several. Industrialized nations seldom war with one another. Because the economy becomes more and more diverse with technology, families become less centered on providing food for themselves. They also become less involved in education and are less involved in religious practices. Instead, scientific knowledge is revered and education of young is left to those thought to be better at it.

- *Post-Industrial Societies:*
  Post-industrial societies use a combination of labor, capital, technology, and raw materials. They develop into interdependent environments. Computers become vitally important as global interconnectedness increases. Education and science are seen as keys to success, and all technological innovations are hailed as valuable commodities. Most problems are centered around the imbalance of resources, financial and political. Those imbalances spread out to environmental concerns as more raw materials are used to meet the demanding needs of a growing population. One primary focus of the post-industrial society is the achievement of equal rights.

As societies progress from one to the next, or stagnate and remain successful at whatever level they are, they interact with the world around them in different ways. They also provide differing social structures and role requirements.

Socialization

Socialization is the process by which individuals learn the roles and structure of their society. In this process of social interactions, individuals also learn what the roles of others should be or are. Strong instincts are lacking in the human race, so socialization helps make up what is lacking in the adaptation process of human young. Just what is learned through socialization? Language, norms, skills, beliefs, values, what is and is not appropriate behavior and thoughts, etc. Each individual in a society also develops a sense of their self-worth through the same process. Is their self-image negative or positive and how much is determined by environment and how much by internal markers is still open to debate.

The process of socialization is lifelong and in a constant state of change. Beginning at birth, most of an individual's socialization has cemented by the end of childhood. Emotional development, a large part of socialization, seems to occur at rather fixed increments, according to recent research. While a newborn has a mere four emotions (pleasure, surprise, disgust, and distress), other emotions soon develop and more continue to develop until the more complex emotions develop in adolescence.

Age	Emotion
Newborn	Pleasure, surprise, disgust, distress
6-8 weeks	Joy
3 months	Anger
8-9 months	Fear
12-18 months	Affection
5-6 years	Insecurity, confidence, envy
Adolescence	More complex emotions

Table 9: Ages of Emotional Development

Traumatic life experiences can hinder or halt the developmental timeline. Common experiences in a societal culture, particular subcultures, family, and friends all play integral roles in the socialization of each member of a society. There are a great many similarities among those in the same society, but differences between subcultures. There are similarities between members of a family or group of friends, but there are differences in each individual.

Personal Development
Personality, the patterns of thought, feeling, and action of an individual, is influenced by socialization. Contrary to the view that personality is unique to an individual, psychologists view personality as a learned or patterned behavior. There are three recognized components of personality:

- Cognitive component: Thoughts, beliefs, perceptions, and other intellectual abilities.
- Emotional aspect: Feelings.
- Behavioral component: Skills, aptitudes, competencies.

The development of a personality and the concept of self are integrated closely to the process of socialization. The concept of self, as defined by sociologists, is a person's awareness of and feelings about his or her social status and identity.

Several theories of personal development have been developed over the course of sociological study and inquiry.

- *Looking Glass Self:*
  Charles Horton Cooley, American economist and social psychologist, declared that concept of self is developed in early childhood and are reevaluated when new social situations are encountered. Cooley's <u>Theory of the Looking Glass Self</u> states that self-concept is developed when an individual evaluates how others look at and react to him or her. This process has three steps:
  1. Individual imagines how behavior seems to others.
  2. Individual interprets the reaction of others to his/her behavior.
  3. Individual utilizes that interpretation to develop self-image or self- concept.

- *Role Taking*

George Herbert Mead, a philosopher and social psychologist who elaborated on the Looking Glass Self theory, argued that children do not, at first, understand that they are separate from others. When they develop language and symbols, they are able to make that cognitive leap and begin to develop self-concepts. Symbolic interaction is the term introduced by Mead that explained how symbols, like signs, gestures, and language, make it possible for people to interact. Language was of particular importance to him. He also argued that it is very important to socialization for individuals to understand what others expect of them.

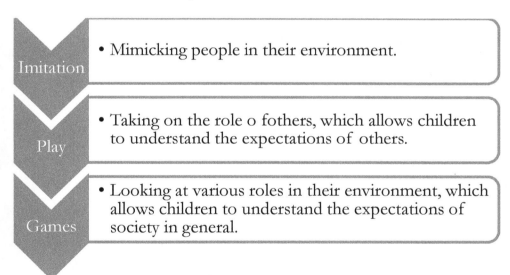

Figure 4: Three Stages of Socialization in Children

- *Emotional Development:*
  Sigmund Freud explained personal development in terms relating to the constant states of conflict between individuals and society. Behavior, in Freud's terms, occurred as the product of nature and nurture. He thought humans were born with certain drives or needs, and emphasized the importance of emotions. In Freud's mind, human personality was

comprised of three parts:

1. <u>Id</u>: Biological and psychological drives (also unconscious memories).
2. <u>Ego</u>: Mediator between id and superego (this ends up being the personality that is ultimately developed).
3. <u>Superego</u>: Censor, conscience, and monitor of personality (opposes the id).

Freud explained that certain outcomes could be hypothesized based on the degree of restrictiveness experienced during childhood. For example, if a child experiences an extremely restrictive environment, their superego will play a more dominant role in personality development. If a child is raised in a freer environment, their id will play a greater role in personality development.

- *Identity Crisis:*

  Erik Erikson was heavily influenced by Freud. He developed eight stages of self-development; each stage is defined by an identity crisis. In this way, Erikson identified with Freud's thought that conflict was central to personal development.

Age	Stage (Central Conflict)
Infancy	Trust vs. mistrust
Early childhood	Autonomy vs. shame/doubt
Preschool age	Initiative vs. guilt
School age	Industry vs. inferiority
Adolescence	Identity vs. role confusion
Young adulthood	Intimacy vs. isolation
Middle age	Generativity vs. stagnation
Old age	Integrity vs. despair

Table 10: Erikson's 8 Stages of Self-Development

- *Cognitive Development:*

  Jean Piaget, through experimentation, developed four stages of cognitive development. He posited that in each stage, individuals learn some key skill(s) or intellectual processes.

Stage	Age	Description
Sensorimotor	Birth-2 years	Intelligence is expressed via physical contact with the environment.
	0-4 months	Infants are not aware of their acts. They do not distinguish themselves from their environment.

	0-8 months	Object permanence has not developed; if they can't see it, they don't think it exists.
	8+ months	Object permanence has developed.
Preoperational	2-7 years	Unable to perform mental operations. No understanding of speed, weight, numbers, quantity, or causality. Egocentric.
Concrete operational	7-12 years	Able to reason about concrete situations. Abstract ideas are still beyond reasoning. Can perform mental operations. Assume roles of others. Participate in social activities.
Formal operational	Adolescence	Achieve formal, abstract thought. Manipulate complex math problems. Reason about moral issues.

Table 11: Piaget's 4 Stages of Cognitive Development

- *Moral Development by Lawrence Kohlberg:*
  Lawrence Kohlberg developed a model of moral development. His model was more sophisticated than Piaget's. His three levels of moral development were divided into six stages.

Level	Description	Stages
Pre-conventional morality	Right and wrong based on punishment or reward.	Stage 1: Obedience orientation Stage 2: Instrumental relativist orientation
Conventional morality	Right and wrong based on laws. Attempting to please others by doing good.	Stage 3: Good boy/nice girl orientation Stage 4: Law and order orientation
Post-conventional morality	Right and wrong based on one's own conscience.	Stage 5: Social contract orientation Stage 6: Universal ethical principle orientation

Agents of Socialization
The influences of socialization that affects individuals throughout the lifespan are agents of socialization. They provide the structured situations in which typical socialization takes place. These include:

- *Family:*
  This is the most significant factor in socialization. Language, emotions, norms, and values are developed within the parameters of the family. Deliberate and unintentional socialization occurs in the family environment. We also get a concrete status as a member of a family.

- *Schools (and daycare centers):*
  This is the first major socialization environment outside the family. This atmosphere provides specific skills, knowledge, and values. Social roles in the school system are broader. Conformity to rules and authority is emphasized.

- *Peers:*
  This refers to individuals of roughly the same age who also share something in common socially, such as grade level or school. Peer groups tend to form accidentally in childhood. In adolescence and adulthood, peer groups are chosen with more thought and direct input. As peer influence increases, parental influence seems to decrease. Peer group socialization has no specific design; it is focused on its own set of interests and concerns. Peer groups are not automatically accepting; some level of conformity is required.

- *Mass Media:*
  The various forms of communication people in today's world come in contact with exposes everyone to differing viewpoints and cultures. More than was ever possible before. While mass media has the potential to provide a positive socialization tool, the themes and content is not always deemed positive by everyone. There is no arguing that mass media, and specifically the Internet, is a prime ground for socialization to take place. Social networking sites, MySpace, Facebook, Twitter, etc. have massive numbers of people subscribed and logging in daily to interact and absorb information.

- *Other Agents:*
  Religious groups and youth organizations are other socialization formats. Resocialization is the process of learning a new set of socially acceptable behaviors that sharply contradicts previous socialization. This is most common in those converting to or from a cult.

> ### *Nature vs. Nurture*
> The classic debate has left many social scientists declaring that it is a combination of both heredity (nature) and environment (nurture) that plays a role in the development of personality and social behavior.
>
> It is now commonly thought that both factors are so inter-related that they cannot be separated or thought of individually.
>
> Nurture is necessary in the positive growth of children. Children are supposed to be cared for and taught.

Socialization through the Lifespan

Socialization is a changing, lifelong process. As status changes, individuals mature and experience new situations, ideas must be formed and processed; self-images must be reevaluated. Lifespan is considered the amalgamation of the following time periods:

- Infancy: Basic motor socialization occurs along with family social structure and bonds developed.
- Childhood: Often referred to as primary socialization because children encounter many new roles and situations.
- Adolescent youth: Abstract thinking begins in this period of new roles and emerging peer influence.
- Mature adulthood: Primary socialization is complete; self-image and values are established.
- Old age: Facing impending death and a decrease in physical stamina, individuals accept lower prestige and lose their self-identity.
- Death: Elizabeth Kubler-Ross developed five stages of dealing with the death.
    - Denial: disbelief.
    - Anger: Asking 'Why Me?'
    - Bargaining: Making deals with a supreme being.
    - Depression: Extreme sadness; being upset.
    - Acceptance: peace of mind with what has happened or what will happen.

- The process of dealing with the loss of a loved one (<u>bereavement</u>) is called mourning. The four phases of mourning are:
    1. Shock (refusing to acknowledge the news)
    2. Protest (refusing to accept the news)
    3. Despair (depression)
    4. Adaptation (accepting and/or beginning to move on and build a new life)

Social Interaction

<u>Social interaction</u> is the process of people reacting and responding to one another. Social interaction is constant as people go about their daily lives with those around them in the various environments they go through. <u>Interactionist perspective</u> contains many viewpoints that all strive to emphasis the interpretation and meaning of life.

- *Symbolic Interaction:*
  George Herbert Mead was one of the first social scientists to study human interactions. He defined an <u>act</u> as a person's total reaction to a situation, including the actual behavior along with all associated feelings. As expressed earlier in the chapter, symbolic interaction uses a symbol that meaningfully represents something. Clothing, signs, and gestures are all valid symbols. Many more exist. The use of symbols relies on all parties being aware of the meaning behind the symbols. It's easy in cross-cultural situations for each party to receive

different messages from symbolic interaction.

- *Dramaturgy:*
Founded by Erving Goffman, the <u>dramaturgical approach</u> analyzes social interactions as if the participants are acting out a play or a scene in a play. It focuses on how people follow the 'script' and/or improvise. According to Goffman, people try to manage the impressions they make on others by creating scenes, called <u>impression management</u>. He states that how a person thinks other view him or her is often different from how that person actually views him/her.

- *Ethnomethodology:*
This approach links dramaturgy to symbolic interaction in its approach. <u>Ethnomethodology</u> refers to how people use commonly understood rules of engagement to dictate how they react in specific situations and thereby be understood by all involved.

- *Conversation analysis:*
Within conversations, there are at least three common characteristics that were first discovered by Harvey Sachs who developed conversation analysis.
    1. Turn-taking
    2. Speaker transitions
    3. Interruptions

- *Social psychology:*
<u>Social psychology</u> is concerned with how personality and behavior is influenced or altered by social contexts. This perspective draws from both sociology and psychology. It utilizes the symbolic interactions view of sociology and the emphasis on experimentation from psychology.

- *Nonverbal communication:*
The exchange of information via nonlinguistic symbols includes many <u>nonverbal communication</u> methods. Humans communicate in this way frequently. Someone may react to how a person stands when speaking just as much as they do to what is being said. The forms of nonverbal communication encompass two types of body language: facial expressions (how the face moves or contorts to reveal emotions) and gestures (how the body moves to express attitude or emotion). Nonverbal communication is also apparent when personal space is manipulated.

Zone	Description
Intimate distance	Intimate physical contact
Personal distance	Reserved for friends and family
Social distance	No physical contact; usually professional, formal situations

Public distance	The outermost distance that is reserved for everyone else in your environment that is part of the general public, not your other circles of influence or camaraderie

Table 12: Hall's 4 Zones of Personal Space

Interaction takes many forms; there are primarily four types:

- Exchange: Possible reward or positive outcome dictates behavior toward others.
- Cooperation: Achieving a common goal that is difficult to achieve as an individual dictates behavior.
- Conflict: Obtaining a prized object or reward dictates behavior, defeat of the opponent is essential.
  - Competition: A type of conflict, but obtaining the goal or prize is more important that defeating the opponent.
- Coercion: The will of one (or a small group) is forced on others, dictating behaviors.

The way individuals react to one another has something to do with whether they are connected in any meaningful way in society. Are they simply citizens of the same country, or do they work together? Are they in love with each other? Are they members of the same social network? Each of those situations would call for entirely different sets of social rules and etiquette.

A social network is a loosely unified group of people whose members interact on occasion and who share a loose sense of identity. Usually they share a common goal or expectation. Social networks are not strongly bound. The typical individual forms many networks throughout their life; each can have a profound impact on status. The primary functions of any social network are:

- To be a primary source of information
- To provide companionship
- To influence decisions and preferences

The term 'networking' refers to meeting the right people in the professional world.

As life progresses, individuals tend to create repetitive patterns of behavior. These are referred to as habits, and they are useful because they enable a person to react to a situation automatically. As society progresses and individuals' habits are observed and perhaps copied, eventually, the habit becomes shared by most or all of a society. It becomes symbolic of that society. An institution is the collection of shared expectations about long-held public habits. Roles are collections of habitual behaviors that are associated with a particular position in a society. In general, when a person assumes a role, they assume those habitual behaviors and society reacts to them based on that role, not as an individual, when in the act of performing that role.

Groups and Organizations

Individuals in society are organized in various ways according to need and preference. For various reasons, groups and organization are formed and reformed, torn apart and restructured.

Groups

A group is two or more people who share common ideas, feelings, and/or pursuits. Members interact with one another based on those norms and according to their common purpose. Most groups have a structure of statuses and roles; this structure can be rigid or flexible. Members share a common sense of belonging and are mutually aware of one another and responsive to each other.

The two basic types of groups are:

- Primary: A small number of people
    - Interact over a long period of time
    - Intimate group interactions
    - Closely bonded
    - Relationships are warm, intimate, and personal
    - Emotional associations
    - Expressive communication

- Secondary: A larger number of people
    - Interact on a temporary basis
    - No intimacy
    - Limited contact
    - Formed for a specific need or a practical purpose
    - Loosely bonded
    - Task-oriented associations

At different sizes, groups have certain characteristics. A small group contains few members; each member is able to relate to one another as individuals. The dyad is the smallest possible group; it contains two people. It is more personal and intense than larger groups. The triad contains three people. It allows for alliances or coalitions and can add a level of pressure to conform. This relationship is less stable that the dyad.

As groups become larger, their dynamics continue to shift. Interactions become more complex. Imbalance can occur as coalitions are formed. Cliques can form of smaller, like-minded, individuals inside the larger group. Communication becomes more formal and norms will shift as new members weigh in on beliefs and appropriate behaviors.

Group Norms and Roles

Norms, again, establish which behaviors are acceptable and which are deviant, both for members inside the group and members acting outside the group. Roles, on the other hand, are spontaneous. Roles are not codified; someone may be the unifier, or the talker, or the idea guy. In most cases, the demands of a group's structure outweigh a person's preferences.

Within a group, there is the phenomenon of people getting along better when they interact more frequently. They find themselves sharing more common values and norms the more they associate together. This is called extent of association.

Leadership within Groups

One of the most important elements within any social structure is leadership. A leader is someone who is able to influence the behavior of others, primarily through personality traits. A leader initiates, directs, organizes, and/or controls what members do and how they think or perceive something. Leaders are present in almost every type of group. They have some common characteristics, such as:

- Height: They are generally taller than everyone else
- Physical attractiveness: In general, they are a version of what looks good to the group members
- Intelligence
- Extroverted with good social and communication skills
- Self-confident
- Determined
- Liberal: More so than other members, at least
- Psychologically balanced

Types of Leaders:
- Instrumental, or task, leader:
  - Organizes group to achieve goals
  - Helps define job
  - Helps determine the best way to achieve goals.

- Expressive leader:
  - Well-liked
  - Creates harmony, keep morale high, minimizes conflict
  - Offers emotional support to achieve solidarity
  - Looks out for emotional well-being of members
  - Relieves tension, possibly by telling a joke

Leadership Styles:
- Authoritarian: Gives orders

- o Not effective because internal conflict is rampant in regime
- o Effective in emergencies
  - Democratic: Acts to win a consensus for his/her plans and ideas
    - o Effective in conflict resolution
    - o Group decision-making
    - o Most effective
  - Laissez-faire: Passive
    - o Provides no direction for group decision-making
    - o Disorganized

Decision-Making within Groups

Groups usually make decisions based on consensus. Discussion is used to bring about a greater level of agreement. Groups are more efficient than single individuals at solving complex problems. They are able to collect more information and analyze the facts more thoroughly. As information is processed and opinions are expressed, reactions and reanalysis occur, leaving the group as a whole more informed and able to make a better decision. While emotional tension can result, after decisions are made, groups generally act toward restoring harmony.

When an individual acts in the best interest of the group and its goals, instead of his own – even if the group's goals are contrary to his own – this is called group conformity. Group pressure, or peer pressure has an immense effect on people; behavior that would otherwise not be considered will be engaged in, simply as a means to 'fit in.' This kind of action can help the group when completing tasks that may seem like drudgery or menial. In order to be a productive member of the group, members will submit to the need and complete the tasks they normally would not have considered.

When making decisions that deal with indeterminate tasks, those with no absolutely correct answer, different groups may not agree on an answer but instead come up with different answers to the same dilemma. Determinate tasks are those that have a definite single answer. In either case, groups have the inherent benefit of having several opinions and the skills and professional knowledge of many members to assist in the decision making process.

There is a negative turn groups can take, though. In two ways, the dynamics of a group can end up causing inappropriate or disastrous decisions. Should the group attempt to reach a conclusion without researching or testing various ideas, groupthink is occurring, and it greatly reduces the effectiveness of the group's ability to produce a positive outcome. Decisions are made using much narrower focus, because the focus is not to make a good decision but to eliminate or avoid conflict.

In some cases, groups make more extreme decisions than each member would have made on his/her own. This is called group polarization. J.A. Stoner hypothesized that such decisions are usually made because of the security of shared responsibility in the case of a wrong decision and because of the cultural applause given to bold decisions.

Group Boundaries

Group boundaries clarify who is a member and who is not. Individuals classify each group they are a member of as an in-group. Those groups they are not involved with are out-groups. Competitions can erupt between groups, and that tension can strengthen group solidarity and group loyalty.

Reference Groups

Reference groups are used a standard for evaluation. An individual's self-evaluation is greatly influenced by the reference group they choose. Personalities and behaviors are strongly influenced by those groups deemed worthy of being used as a reference point.

Networks

Social networks are links between individuals who interact continually in some capacity. Networks are vital to societies and are made up of primary contacts (family and close friends) and secondary contacts (co-workers, professional acquaintances). A person's sense of community relies on his or her network, how large or small it is.

Organizations

An organization is a large, formal association. Organizations can be closed or have limited admission. Generally, the relationships in this kind of association are secondary and impersonal. Modern society is full of named organizations that have an official purpose or goal(s); they have statuses and roles, and expect members to follow a set of rules to promote those goals.

Amitai Etzioni characterized the three broadest types of organizations:

1. Voluntary: People are free to join and leave as they become interested in the group's purposes.
2. Utilitarian: Members join such organizations for practical reasons, usually for some gain.
3. Coercive: Individuals are forced to participate.

Organizations are very structured, unlike primary groups. Each formal organization has the following:

- Informal structure: Personal interactions between members, improving the efficiency of the organization.
- Organizational culture: Important to success, the well-defined identity, clear values, heroes, rites and rituals bring order to the work of the organization.
- Cultural network: Hidden hierarchy that obtains and spreads information.

Bureaucracies

A bureaucracy is a hierarchical authority structure with strict rules and procedures. Though they are often thought to be negative, bureaucracies can be very efficient because of their structure. Karl Marx disliked them, calling them an unnecessary evil. Max Weber analyzed bureaucracies and provided a demonstration of their efficiency. He realized that they were a form of rationalization; traditional, spontaneous methods were replaced by carefully selected codes and procedures.

Weber provided ideal types, descriptions based on several cases that illustrate the essential features. The six essential features he defined were:

1. Division of labor: Clearly defined and determined; each member has a specialized job.
2. Hierarchy: Pyramid-shaped; greater authority at the top; top-down chain of command.
3. Regulations & formal rules: Specific, official, and written; used to govern all daily functions.
4. Impersonality & universalism: Evaluation and reward based on performance; no special favors.
5. Record keeping: Comprehensive; standardized.
6. Managerial or administrative staff: Specialized staff to keep the organization running smoothly.
7. Lifelong careers: Possible to climb the ladder to higher positions; seniority promoted.

With all the positives of the bureaucracy states thus far, it must be noted that there are two specific criticisms:

1. Parkinson's Law: In a bureaucracy, work tends to expand to fill the time allotted for it.
2. Peter Principle: In a hierarchy, every employee tends to rise (or fall) to his/her level of incompetence.

Other, less specific, complaints with bureaucracies include their inefficiency when dealing with abnormal problems. They are created to deal with the usual, not the unusual. Another major complaint is called bureaucratic enlargement, the tendency for all bureaucracies to grow. It is also argued that the pressure to conform stifles creativity, greatly reducing the overall effectiveness.

Oligarchy

Oligarchy refers to an organization that is ruled by a hierarchy with a few powerful individuals at the top. In general, it is thought that bureaucracies lead to oligarchies. Robert Michel's Iron Law of Oligarchy states that no matter how democratic and organization attempts to be, it ultimately is the leaders that are running the organization.

In main problem faced by oligarchic organizations is that decision making cannot be left to the masses. Leaders tend to be persuasive and powerful and have access to knowledge. This allows them to control information flow, possibly keeping lower-level members out of the loop. Members tend to look up to the leaders; they also have less commitment to their job and are usually more than willing to leave the big decisions to their leader. Because leaders want to keep their positions (and the associated power), they tend to promote those who are loyal to them. These factors lead to oligarchy.

Collective Organizations

Collective organizations consist of part-time volunteers who contribute to many of the necessary aspects of an organization, including decision making.

Becoming Institutionalized

Organizations change just as the individuals within them do – as a natural progression of growth; often, internal power struggles (shifts, leadership breakdown, worker protests) and external factors (new technology, new markets, changing values, competition) are the leading causes of that growth.

Organizations become institutionalized when the following is established:

- Loyal members are recruited
- Goals are achieved efficiently
- Larger community is accepting
- Stable structure, complete with goals and values, is established

Becoming institutionalized provides a more rigid structure and stability; it may also cause members to fear for their role, taking their focus off of the overall goals of the organization (goal displacement). Knowledge and experience blossom under institutionalism.

Today's Changes

Rigid bureaucratic structures are becoming less common as flexible, democratic organizations grow in number. These types of businesses encourage new designs and changes; they also have a diffusion of power, not a concentration of it. Flexible organizations offer flex time and job sharing. Flex time grants workers flexibility in their schedule as an expanded number of acceptable hours is offered. Job sharing grants part-time employees the ability to see to their family's needs while simultaneously continuing their careers.

Deviance and Social Control

Deviance is behavior that violates social norms and expectations and results in the disapproval of a large group of people. Contrary to conformity, which helps to stabilize society, deviance works against, or disrupts, social structure. Most individuals have deviated from the norm at some point in their lives. It is even possible that one behavior is accepted in one situation and not in a completely different situation.

Although deviance is usually considered to be negative, it doesn't have to be; it could simply be an act that is not commonly evidenced in a society, such as something that is more heroic than normal. A stigma, a characteristic much like a 'mark' that is shared by deviants and sets them apart from 'normal' members of society. For example, the stigma of going to jail continues to follow a person as they   apply   for   jobs.

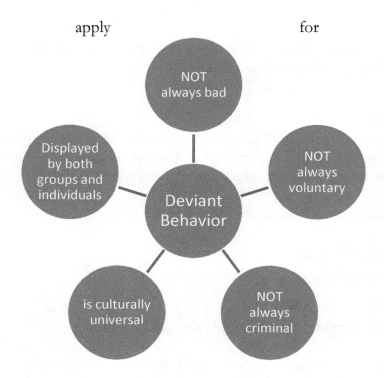

Figure 5: What is Deviance?

Deviant behavior is not always bad; it could just be a sign of nonconformity (for example, bikers). Deviant behavior is not always voluntary; it could just be a sign of physical limitation (for example, being handicapped). Deviant behavior is also not always criminal; the above examples are perfect illustrations of this. Emile Durkheim even argued that deviance is an integral part of healthy societies. He stated that some level of deviance actually provides an outline of acceptable behaviors, strengthen group solidarity, and bring about social change. Both individuals and groups can act in defiance of the norms. For example, a group that stands in opposition to a popular statute is exhibiting deviant behavior.

When most parts of the population are in a state of conformity to the established norms of the society, social order exists. This is only possible with an effective means of social control in place to ensure that generally acceptable behaviors are exhibited. Measures of social control aim to encourage conformity and discourage deviance. Socialization is the beginning of social control and ensures that individuals internalize social norms. Most people conform without even thinking about it; it is natural.

There are two types of social control. They each attempt to restrain deviant behavior, but each come from different sources.

1. Internal controls: conscience, values, integrity, morality, and the desire to be good.
2. External controls: police, family, friends, and religion.

Deviance, ultimately, is a failure of social control, whether that is a failure of an individual's internal controls or society's external controls. <u>Sanctions</u> provide rewards for conformity and punishment for nonconformity. External controls can include both formal and informal sanctions. <u>Informal sanctions</u> are those imposed by primary group and involve disapproval or rejection for nonconformity; they are often vague, but they are very effective. <u>Formal sanctions</u> are those imposed by organizations or entities and involve specific punishments (like law enforcement sentencing you to jail time).

Perspectives

Many perspectives have been explored to explain and help societies understand their makeup and the tendency of some to fall into deviance. What one generation or culture finds deviant is not necessarily what the next generation or a different culture will think of as deviant. Think of television standards, for example; they have gradually worsened. What is viewed today would be considered deviant offerings one generation ago.

Biological Perspectives:

In general, the earliest research on a link between behavior and biology were inconclusive. Modern research continues on the quest to find any biological component to deviance; if one exists, social scientists are determined to find it.

1. Medicalization: Asserts that deviance is a result of physical or mental illness. (For example, drunkenness is now not a moral failure, but a "disease of alcoholism.")
    1. Attempts to find any pathological reason for deviance.
2. Theory of atavism: Cesare Lombroso. States that deviant behavior is inherited.
    1. Certain genetic traits reappear in later generations (atavism).
    2. This provides, theoretically, a means of identifying deviant types.
3. Body type theory: William Sheldon. Claims that criminal behavior is based on general body types (somatotypes).
    1. The claim is that a relationship exists between body type, psychological state, and criminal behavior.
        - The three major body types include:
1. Endomorph: Rounded body, tendency to gain weight, short limbs combined with a relaxed, extroverted personality.
2. Ectomorph: Small, delicate bones, lean, low body mass combined with introversion and a tendency to fatigue easily and complain.
3. Mesomorph: Muscular, large boned combined with aggression and assertiveness.
    - XYY theory: The idea that an additional male chromosome leads to aggression or deviance.
    - Proven to exist in those within the prison population and mental hospitals to a higher degree than the general population.

Psychological Perspectives:

It is thought by many sociologists that certain personality types are more likely to commit deviant behavior than others. A Freudian explanation would be that the id and ego are unbalanced or that the superego lacks the strength to overcome the id.

- Eysenck's thoughts: Stated that no one was born deviant, but could be genetically prone to it.
  - Believes that extroverts are more prone to deviant behaviors because of their riskier behavior, in general.
- Bandura's thoughts: Stated that all deviance is learned by observation and imitation.
- Berkowitz's thoughts: Developed <u>frustration-aggression hypothesis</u> which states that aggressive behavior is a sign of previous frustrations; those previous frustrations lead to aggressive behavior, either overt or covert.
  - Based on psychoanalytic explanations of aggression and physiological emotion theories.
  - Many do not think this theory adequately explains the wide range of aggressive behavior that is known.

Sociological Perspectives:

Sociologists examine why deviance occurs, its pattern(s), and why certain behaviors are classified as deviant and others are not.

1. Cultural transmission theory: states that deviance is learned through interactions, in the same manner that conformity is learned.
   - Shaw and McKay examined Chicago's highest crime zones and found that adolescents learned deviant behavior from their environment, especially through their play groups and gangs.
   - Sociologists assert that some environments meant to correct deviance, like prisons, actually teach it.
2. Differential association: Edwin Sutherland. Cultural transmission occurs through social relationships oriented toward certain populations. For example, drug addicts relapse because they reenter networks in which that behavior is the norm.
   - Primary groups are the location of this learned behavior model, making it hard to escape and even harder to move out of.
   - Explains that what is deviant in the main culture may be acceptable in a subculture.
3. Structural strain theory: Robert Merton. Explains the widespread deviance in certain portions of society.
   - Portions of society that experience less opportunity for improvement resort to deviance. In other words, deviance is a result of a society's imbalance, or the added strain placed on some within a society.
   - The phrase "poverty breeds crime" derives from this theory.
   - Emile Durkheim introduced the term <u>anomie</u>, a state of confusion or imbalance that exists when norms are weak, absent, or conflicting. Durkheim insisted that modern

culture is especially prone to developing anomie because of the diversity of cultures. The diversity creates confusion about norms and values; moral guidelines are not clearly defined in such environments.

- Anomie arise when socially approved goals outnumber the socially approved ways of obtaining those goals. There are five ways, according to Merton, for people to react to such a discrepancy.
    1. Conformity: Culturally approved methods are utilized to obtain culturally approved goals. This is the most common response.
    2. Innovation: Approved goals are achieved using unapproved, immoral, or illegal methods. This is the most common type of deviance.
    3. Ritualism: Approved goals are viewed as irrelevant but still sought out.
    4. Retreatism: Approved goals and means are abandoned. This is viewed by society as a double failure.
    5. Rebellion: Approved goals and means are rejected. New, unapproved goals and methods of achieving them are adopted.
- Merton places the blame for deviance on society's structure and culture.

4. Labeling theory (Symbolic interactionist view): Asserts that deviance is a process that allows some in a society to classify others as deviants.
    - Focuses on how a person comes to be titled deviant.
    - In this theory, a person is only a deviant when they are labeled thusly. It is the way a person is labeled, not the act, which these sociologists examine.
        - Primary deviance is related to unique situations (social, cultural, psychological). These behaviors do no alter a person's self-concept as they are not internalized. Examples: shoplifting for thrill, sipping alcohol before 21.
        - Secondary deviance evolves from self-concept. Behaviors stem from identification with the label placed on them by others. They internalize the label and act accordingly. Example: A teen stealing because he is thief.
    - Empirical evidence suggests that labeling is not influential in the case of deviance.

5. Control theory: Explains deviance as a result of the failure of social control.
    - Asks the question of why people conform in the first place.
    - Believes that people understand right and wrong, but reject environmental causes for criminal behavior.
    - The more integrated an individual is into his/her community, the less likely they are to commit a deviant behavior.
        - Strong bonds make deviance costly to the individual.
        - Weak bonds free a person to deviate; there is no cost or little cost to deviance.

6. Social control theory: Travis Hirschi. In this theory of criminal behavior, the focus is on why people abstain from committing crimes.
    - In general, it is society's moral code that provides the reason. Hirschi details four moral bonds that control deviant behavior:

- Attachment to others: specifically parents and peers
- Commitment: goals would be sacrificed for deviance
- Involvement: time constraints restrict available time to be deviant
- Belief: conventional moral codes

7. Self-control theory: Hirschi and Michel Gottfredson. Claims that people are unable to control impulses; they lack self-control and are unable to put off gratification, thus deviance occurs.
8. Containment theory: Walter Reckless. States that criminals lack a positive self-concept which makes them unable to resist temptations.
9. Becker's thoughts: states that most people's behavior is a result of the consequences of a previous deviant act.
   - A primary deviation leads to secondary deviation.
10. Conflict theory: Asserts that not every member in a community share identical values.
    - Small, powerful groups have values and goals that are different from those of the less powerful groups. Thus, some actions of the less powerful seem to be deviant to those in power.
    - Culture conflict theory: Every society contains smaller subcultures with their own set of values and norms.
    - Marxian conflict theory: The inequalities of American life cause deviance.

Based on the above theories, the three steps to becoming a career deviant include:

1. Observe a deviant act by someone in the primary group (Differential association theory)
2. Have a label assigned (Labeling theory)
3. Join a deviant subculture

Crime and Statistics

Crime is an act that contradicts a formal law and is punishable by negative sanctions. Illegal behaviors are those that are considered to be too socially disruptive and/or too difficult to control through informal sanctions. The law defines the nature of the offense, states who cannot perform that act, and describes the sanction applicable.

The Federal Bureau of Investigation classifies crimes into four categories.

- Violent crimes: Committed against persons; these are the most serious crimes; murder, rape
- Crimes against property: Burglary and theft
- Crimes without victims: Moral crimes; prostitution
- White collar (corporate) crimes: Committed by the powerful for money; embezzlement

Organized crime refers to the act of making a profit off of illegal activities. Violent crimes only account for 1-2% of all crime, but they receive the most attention because of the severity.

The FBI compiles information concerning eight index crimes. Those index crimes are: homicide, forcible rape, aggravated assault, robbery, larceny-theft, burglary, auto theft, and arson. Generalized statistics are available based on the information gathered. Variations in the statistics occur.

- Most crime is committed by those 25 years old or younger
- Males commit most crime
- Crime rates are higher in the black population than in the white population
- Large cities have higher crime rates than smaller communities
- Urban areas have more reported crime than rural areas

Many crimes remain unreported because victims may have a fear of retribution or a low expectation of police ability. A victim may refrain from reporting a crime if a family member is involved in that crime. The more serious a crime, however, the more likely it is to be reported.

Sociological factors influence crime. For example, during WW2, crime rates were lower in the US because many men were at war. During the population explosion after WW2, crime increased a dramatic 200%. The factors commonly pointed to for the increase in crime are: higher youth population, television violence, poverty, and drug use.

Criminal Justice System
Identifying criminals is a several stage process. At each stage, the alleged criminal has only a chance of moving on to the next stage. That chance greatly increasing with the severity of the crime and the social status of the offender.

Figure 6: Criminal Justice System Process

The criminal justice system involves the police, courts, and state and national correctional systems.

- o The police are supposed to control crime. They are under almost constant public scrutiny.
  They face danger daily, and this often affects their attitudes.
  - Officers are taught how and when to apply different types of force:
    - Legal force: To take someone into custody.
    - Normal force: Specific to circumstances.

- Excessive force: Completely unnecessary and brutal.
  o The highly complex court system is supposed to determine guilt or innocence of the accused, as well as any punishment.
    - Plea bargaining: Negotiating guilty pleas to lesser crimes.
      - This occurs more frequently in an effort to reduce the costs associated with jury trials.
    - Corrections: The sanctions sentenced by the judge. These include imprisonment, probation, and parole.
  o The correctional systems are supposed to apply the sanctions given by the courts.
    - There are four purposes of the correctional facility:
      - Retribution: Punishment
      - Deterrent: To keep the criminal and others from thinking about crime
      - Incapacitation: Restrict the criminal's freedom
      - Rehabilitate: Provide skill training to help offender become law-abiding
    - The rate of recidivism, repeated crime, is high. Resource limitations keep prisons from concentrating on rehabilitation. An environment ripe with new criminal knowledge offers another challenge to rehabilitation.

Crime and the Conflict Perspective

Looking for a conflict, the relationship between deviants and their accusers is examined. Whose law and order is upheld by the legal sanctions? Each group has their own interests and conflict is imminent. Marx, of course, asserts that laws support the powerful over the weak and the rich over the poor. It is argued that crime is behavior that powerful groups consider to be a threat (to their positions and authority).

Mental Disorders:

A psychological inability to handle ordinary situations can be considered a form of deviance, because people with a <u>mental disorder</u> violate norms consistently. From irrational speech and thoughts to delusions and hallucinations, their behavior is unpredictable and certainly does not fall within what the society at large would condone as acceptable.

The causes of most mental disorders are unknown. Some result from physical brain damage, but often, no observable physical cause is apparent. Thomas Szasz argued that mental illness is a myth; he asserted that the behavior is not an illness but a defective means of coping – a mislearned ability.

The highest rates of mental disorder are found in the lowest social classes. The reasons for this are hotly debated. The additional stress of living at or near poverty can make them more susceptible to mental disorder. Another theory is being lower class increases the likelihood of being labeled as mentally ill.

<u>Psychosis</u> is a profound mental disturbance or break with reality that renders the individual unable to function appropriately in society. Psychosis includes extreme paranoia (delusions of

grandeur or persecution), manic-depression (dramatic mood shifts), schizophrenia (intellectual and emotional disengagement).

Deviance has its place in society, but it is also disruptive to society.

Sexuality and Society

Sociologists rejected sexuality as a legitimate research topic until after World War II, even though sexuality has played a significant part in society, whether in the formation or deviations of the population. Sexual acts, feelings, and thoughts are a constant part of life. Sex affects marriage, a classic institution, which leads to the creation of families – a necessity for every society. In effect, society has always regulated sexual behavior.

Kingsley Davis was one of the first sociologists to study sexuality. He thought that sexual behavior is a learned behavior; he thought that socialization played a large part in a person's internalizing the appropriate sexual actions. He hypothesized that individuals are born with powerful sexual drives and through norms and taboos, individuals are guided to appropriate behavior. The appropriateness of sexual activities is social in nature; human sexuality is flexible and societies tend to reflect the majority thoughts on what is right and what is wrong. Different cultures show a large variation of what is practiced, especially in preindustrial societies. There are, however, similar norms or <u>cultural universals</u> found in every society studied.

- o <u>Incest taboos</u>, powerful moral prohibitions against sexual relations between certain relatives.
- o Institution of marriage: It is within this institution that every society expects sexual behavior to be expressed.
  - Marriage is defined as a socially acceptable arrangement between two people.
  - Marriage helps regulate sexual relations, ensures legitimate birth, and provides for a balanced socialization of children with a two-parent household.
  - 2/3 of selected societies forbid adultery.
- o Heterosexuality: Every society indicates at least some conformity to heterosexuality in order to reproduce.
  - 1/3 of societies forbid homosexuality.
  - 2/3 tolerate or approve of homosexuality in a small number of the population.

Beauty and attractiveness standards vary greatly between societies. Societies also differ in their sexual restrictiveness and sexual permissiveness. Sexual restrictiveness refers to an adherence to a narrow definition of sexual norms. Sexual permissiveness refers to an acceptance of greater freedom in sexual norms and behavior.

Norms relating the specifics of the sex act, as can be imagined, are also greatly varied. From position, degree of nakedness, and locations, each culture has their own idea of acceptable and not.

Sex in the United States
In the United States, sexual behavior is markedly different between real and ideal norms. Restrictive traditions coupled with an atmosphere of freedom creates tension. Traditional values that placed sexual conduct in the sole realm of reproduction and the loose application of restrictions on males while females bore the brunt of restrictiveness, has led to an aggravating cultural environment. The double standard was exacerbated as women were degraded for having pre-marital sex and men were elevated, their behavior condoned and encouraged.

Alfred Kinsey conducted the first and, arguably, the most reliable research on American sexual behavior in the 1940s and 1950s. It was his work that indicated the gap between traditional moral norms and real behavior. The 1960s and 1970s brought a sexual revolution and increased permissive behaviors. Ideas concerning premarital sex, the double standard, teenage pregnancy, pornography, and sexually transmitted diseases were changing. Since the sexual revolution, many changes have occurred:

- An increase in premarital sex
- Greater participation by women in sexual activities
- Erosion of the double standard
- Increase in teen pregnancy
  - Many think this is due not only to the increase in permissiveness but also to the lack of readily available contraceptive measures.
- Increase in pornography
- More intense and controversial pornographic content
  - Many believe that pornography, directly or indirectly, causes sex crimes.
  - Evidence has shown men who view pornography to act more callous toward women.
- Increase in the occurrence of STDs

At the end of the sexual revolution, public opinion had actually shifted to show:

- More tolerance for sexual diversity
- Less tolerance for promiscuity
- More commitment to marital fidelity
- Judgment concerning sexual behavior to be more greatly based on affection and respect

Incest
The incest taboo, as mentioned earlier, is a cultural universal. However, it is not instinctive; it is sociological. According to the most recent studies, the incest taboo has evolved over time as a vital need to the health and survival of families. Three reasons for this development across cultures are evidenced here:

1. Early societies, to form alliances, encouraged marriage across borders, so to speak, in

order to strengthen the ties between the two allied groups.

2. Family roles confusion would ensue without an incest taboo. Which role was that woman to play, the wife, the mother, the child?

3. It also prevented sexual jealousies between family members, which could reasonably tear apart a family.

Rape

Rape is considered to be the forcible act of sexual intercourse with an unwilling victim. Rape is a crime of violence, not passion. It has been deemed a demoralizing humiliation and power ritual. It is viewed as socially inappropriate, but it originates in approved patterns of interaction between the genders.

Women often suffer long-lasting psychological distress because of the brutality and invasiveness of the crime. Personal, social, and sexual relations are upset because of the trauma. Sadly, only 1/10 of all rapes are reported because victims do not desire to relive the trauma which is likely to haunt them for the rest of their life.

Many societies, including the United States, are characterized by two elements that are relevant to the prevalence of rape.

- Inequality of men and women
- Tendency for men to view women as sexual objects

The workplace can be home to degrading sexual harassment. While men may feel women are flattered by their advances and comments, they (the men) are only showing their lack of self-control.

Rape is an extreme act of domination. It is not a sudden impulse; it does not happen because no other sexual outlet exists; it is not even sexual in nature. Rapists desire to feel better about themselves by demeaning another.

Homosexuality

Occurring throughout history, homosexuality has taken different forms. From pederasty, homosexuality, and lesbianism, much controversial research has been done on the topic. Pederasty involves the relationship of an adult male and an adolescent boy outside of his family. The ancient Greeks practiced this, as did many other cultures through history, but modern industrial societies shun the practice and make it illegal. Homosexuality is the terms used to signify a relationship between same-sex individuals, both of them consenting adults. Lesbianism refers specifically to female homosexual relations.

Western culture has long stigmatized homosexuality. That is lessening as the years progress. Several theories have been developed as a means of attempting to understand the origin of homosexuality in an individual. Those theories include:

- o Childhood experiences (especially seduction experiences)
- o Family environment (pathological family interactions)
- o Social learning (rewards and punishments)
- o Self-labeling (labeling yourself as gay)
- o Biological/genetic predisposition (gay gene/brain studies)

Controversy still surrounds the issue of whether homosexual couples should enjoy the same rights as heterosexual couples do. The prejudice and discrimination acted on by homophobic individuals is disgraceful to an entire society, no matter what someone's viewpoint is.

Prostitution

Prostitution involves exchanging money for sexual acts. Four forms of prostitution exist:

1. Women for men
2. Men for men
3. Women for women
4. Men for women

The latter two are rare. Male prostitution is evident in larger cities, but the vast majority of prostitutes are female.

This well-established institution has been around for centuries. In ancient Greece, they were called hetaerae and were known to be public companions of rich and powerful men. Other cultures used prostitution as a religious ritual. In modern, western cultures, though, prostitutes are of low social status and work in brothels or solicit clients in public places.

There have been historical movements to rid societies of these women, but it has lasted through all those attempts. Legalized prostitution in the United States is strongly opposed on the ground that it would lessen social morality, legitimize and encourage the practice.

Sociologists have studied prostitution and the different types of theorists all have an idea on why the profession even exists.

- *Functionalist perspective:*
  - These theorists see prostitution as having an effect on society that contributes to the maintenance of the whole society.
  - Explains prostitution as meeting sexual needs without placing too much strain on the family system.

- *Conflict perspective:*
  - These theorists view prostitution as a reflection of the power struggles and relationships within society.

- It benefits the men and exploits the women.
- Prostitution is seen as a reflection of wider inequalities between the sexes.

- *Interactionist perspective:*
  - These theorists view the relationship in question and look at how they interact and understand their own behavior.
  - Considers the socialization of prostitutes.

Chapter Review

Activity 1: Multiple Choice
Identify the correct answer to the question.

1. When people view their own culture as the superior culture, they would be considered:
    A. Ethnocentric
    B. Biased
    C. Racist
    D. Agreeable

2. The most advanced type of society is which one of the following?
    A. Hunting and gathering
    B. Post-apocalyptic
    C. Post-industrialized
    D. Agrarian

3. An ascribed status would be which one of the following?
    A. Professor
    B. Father
    C. Race
    D. Graduate

4. Institutions usually tend to be:
    A. Independent
    B. In constant turmoil
    C. Avoiding social change
    D. Resistant to change

5. Socialization causes _____.
    A. Individuals to learn norms, values, and skills
    B. No change to a person's personality
    C. Temporary results
    D. An increase in conflict

6. How people construct and share their definitions of reality in their everyday interactions is studied in:
    A. Dramaturgy
    B. Ethnomethodology
    C. Socialization
    D. Social psychology

7. Hunting and gathering societies rely on:
   A. Vegetation
   B. Wild animals
   C. Tools
   D. Both A and B

8. Horticultural societies rely on:
   A. Plants
   B. Fresh water fish, not salt water fish
   C. Herd animals
   D. None of the above

9. The process of unlearning old values and behaviors to adopt new ones is called _____.
   A. Disentrainment
   B. Reconditioning
   C. Resocialization
   D. Socialization

10. What is an aggregate?
    A. A farming community
    B. Extended family, especially at the same function
    C. People who happen to be at the same place at the same time
    D. A family

11. What is an example of a primary group?
    A. Co-workers
    B. Family
    C. University campus
    D. Governmental body

12. Which of the following features is a part of bureaucracies, according to Weber?
    A. Impersonality
    B. Clearly defined set of regulations
    C. Division of labor
    D. All of the above

13. What is the set of linked relationships between individuals or social units called?
    A. Social category
    B. Primary group
    C. Secondary group
    D. Social network

14. Which sociologist studied bureaucracies and identified the essential elements present in the ideal types?
    A. DuBois
    B. Parsons
    C. Weber
    D. Marx

15. The current definitions of deviance are the same as they have always been.
    A. True
    B. False

16. Which of the following would be considered a deviant community?
    A. Fraternity
    B. Gang
    C. Police Force
    D. Daycare

17. Behaviors that are sanctioned, or made illegal, are those that:
    A. Are too socially disruptive
    B. Are socially controllable
    C. Are internally controlled
    D. Are controlled by informal sanctions

18. Thomas Szasz believes what about mental disorder?
    A. It is a biochemical imbalance
    B. It is higher than reported in upper classes
    C. It is genetically inherited
    D. It is a myth

19. The social disgrace suffered by a deviant that sets him or her apart from 'normal' members of society is called what?
    A. Internalization
    B. Myth
    C. Stigma
    D. Conformity

20. Negotiating a guilty plea to a lesser crime is a _____.
    A. Plea bargain
    B. Nolo contendere
    C. Sanction
    D. Correction

21. Which sociologist provided the research to confirm that there is a gap between traditional sexual norms and actual sexual norms?
    A. Marx

B. Freud
C. Kinsey
D. Pliney

Activity 2: Short Answer

Answer the questions or prompts as fully as possible using the knowledge you have gained in this chapter.

1. What is the difference between culture and society?

2. What is a subculture?

3. What do values represent?

4. List the four stages of Piaget's cognitive development theory.

5. What are the five stages of dealing with death? Which social scientist identified these stages?

6. What are the four primary types of interaction?

7. Describe the four types of groups.

8. What is the definition of deviance?

9. What is the difference between informal and formal sanction?

10. List the three cultural universals regarding sexuality.

Chapter Review Answers

Activity 1:

1. A
2. C
3. C
4. D
5. A
6. B
7. D
8. A
9. C
10. C
11. B
12. D
13. D
14. C
15. B
16. B
17. A
18. D
19. C
20. A
21. C

Activity 2:

1. Society is a group of socially inter-related people, people who share a common culture; a culture is the sum of output of a society, both material and nonmaterial products.
2. A subculture is a group that shares the overall larger culture, but which differs from the main culture with its own values, norms, and lifestyle.
3. Values are the socially agreed on ideas concerning what is good, right, and desirable. Values are also abstract ideas that express the norms of a society.
4. Sensorimotor, preoperational, formal operation, concrete operational
5. Denial, anger, bargaining, depression, acceptance. Elizabeth Kubler-Ross first discovered and labeled these stages.
6. Exchange, cooperation, conflict or competition, and coercion.
7. Primary group is the closest set that is made up of individuals who interact constantly. Secondary group is made up of those who interact on a temporary basis; it is less personal. Dyad is a two member group. Triad is a three-member group.
8. Deviance is a behavior that violates a society's norms and expectations; it results in the disapproval of a large portion of the population.
9. Informal sanctions are applied by the primary group; they are very effective, but also vague. Formal sanctions are imposed by external organizations.
10. Incest taboos, sexual relations inside of marriage, and conformity to heterosexuality.

Chapter 4: Social Stratification

What's the point?

- To comprehend what social stratification involves.
- To understand the sociological implications of class analysis.
- To identify gender roles.
- To understand racism and its manifestations.
- To properly define classes in American society.
- To grasp the difference between prejudice and discrimination.
- To recognize aging and the issues that are involved in the process.

Every society is stratified, or arranged by levels. Those levels often revolve around income, status, and power, but other factors can be used. Max Weber called these stratifications the economic dimension, social prestige dimension, and political dimension respectively. Each level represents one <u>class</u>, or portion of people who share common relationships and means of production or sources of wealth.

<u>Social status</u> is a socially defined position, or ranking, in a society's stratification system. In modern urban societies, it is harder to determine the status of individuals. Certain <u>status symbols</u>, objects or speech that is associated with a certain status, can help determine such, but are not always accurate indicators. Occupations have historically been the most reliable means of measuring status.

<u>Status consistency</u> refers to the tendency of people who rank high in one area, ranking high in another area (education and wealth, for example). <u>Status inconsistency</u> occurs when individuals rank high in one status area and low in another (like ministry and low income).

Power and Social Inequality

Social inequality exists because of those dimensions. The very idea of stratification means some factor is unequal to all others. Different levels of stratification have inherent expectations or differential treatments expected of others toward those in that category. For example, the young and the old are treated differently in most cultures. Male and female differences usually result in some kind of differing cultural expectations and experiences. The rich and the poor are also treated differently in most cultures. The most basic definition of <u>social inequality</u>, then, is treatment that differs according to age, sex, race, religion, sexual orientation, or education and social rewards are unequally shared. This can take the form of unfair distribution of wealth, status, or power.

Stratification is the structured inequality that classifies groups of people according to their access to a society's reward. Their access to society's rewards is closely determined to their position in the social hierarchy. People within the same stratum, or level of stratification, usually experience the same number of opportunities.

Many social researchers realize that stratification systems tend to rank a person as more deserving of power, wealth, and prestige, which then ensures that hierarchical thinking and models persist. The inequality rests in the fact that individuals are treated according to their social status, not their merit or conduct, in many cases.

Marxists see wealth as the only key to social class stratification. They view societies as only having two distinct classes, those who 'have' and those who 'have not.' The bourgeoisie, or ruling class, land owners, 'haves', monetary controllers, are the upper and dominant class. They exploit the lower, or proletariat, class, the workers who make up the majority of a population. Class conflict erupts because of the differences between the two factions. An ideology is a set of beliefs that helps to explain the arrangement of society. Marx's ideology then relies on the ruling class and its justification of their own economic gains.

Social Mobility

In some societies, it is possible to move or adjust one's social status. In a closed system, ascribed statuses are primary and there is very little chance for a person to change their status. In this type of system, individuals have very little influence on their ranking. In an open system, however, achieved statuses allow individuals to have influence over the social status that they attain. Open systems offer the opportunity to change statuses.

Sociologists have categorized three main types of stratification systems. These systems vary in their mobility.

- Caste system: A closed for that utilizes clearly defined class boundaries.
  - Status is determined at birth (ascribed status) and remains for the duration of life.
  - Endogamy, marriage within the same social class, is required.
  - Ritual pollution, contact between members of different castes, is avoided as much as possible, ensuring that castes stay physically and socially separate and distinct.
- Estate system: Popular in the Middle Ages during feudalism, members of each 'estate' or class are given more privileges than those in lower estates.
  - Offers slightly more mobility than caste system, but is still determined based on the ascribed status of being born as a landowner or not.

- ▪ Status based primarily on land ownership; highest estates own land and all lower estates work for those.
- • Class system: Primarily based on economic status, dependent on income and occupation.
  - ▪ This is the most commonly utilized socialization structure in today's modern world.
  - ▪ It offers the most mobility since membership is based on achieved statuses.
  - ▪ Generally the availability of education and inheritance among wealthy families ensures that the inequality that exists perpetuates.

Class divisions, real and perceived differences between classes, exist when rewards are different between classes, when members are aware of those differences, and when the ability and opportunity to move to a better class is limited.

Social mobility is the upward or downward movement from one social class to another. There are several types of movement:

- • Upward mobility: Aided by industrial development and education; seen as a product of geographic mobility and urbanization.
- • Downward mobility: Caused by a lack of those things that lead to upward mobility, like formal education.
- • Horizontal mobility: Involves a social change while retaining the same social status.
- • Intergenerational mobility: How an individual's status compares to his or her parents'.
- • Intragenerational mobility: How an individual's status changes during the course of his or her life.
- • Structural mobility: Caused by changes in the economy and not due to individual achievement.
- • Exchange mobility: Occurs when people at different hierarchical levels exchange places.

Theories Concerning Social Mobility

Several theories have been put forth, as always in science, to explain phenomenon. The following theories each have their strengths and rely on at least one tenant that is thought by the majority of social thinkers to be acceptable or truthful.

Conflict Theory:

Karl Marx put forth the idea that class conflict hastens social change; that is the true end purpose behind stratification. As much as the ruling class wants to maintain the status quo, the lower classes want to change the prevailing inequalities.

Ralf Dahrendorf thought too much emphasis was placed on class. He instead focused on the struggle between groups like unions and employers.

Randall Collins concentrated on the way different groups maintained their social positions be acquiring education credentials.

Functionalist Theory:

Kingsley Davis and Wilbert Moore argue that stratification functions positively in society. It motivates people and therefore meets society's need for productivity. Because some jobs are more critical for the success of the society, functionalists argue that those jobs should be attached to greater rewards and higher status. Social stability relies on inequality; stratification is a means of matching the most important roles with those who will fulfill them the best.

One major criticism of this theory is that stratification systems do not always work in this manner. A common example of this is professional athletes. Their roles are not vital to the survival of society, but they are paid more than almost everyone else on the planet. Two negative effects of stratification are 1) talent of many is wasted as there is only room in the output for so many to be in those favored positions, and 2) strain.

Lenski's Theory:

Gerhard Lenski saw that parts of functionalist and conflict viewpoints were valid. Lenski noted that functionalism explained only the necessity for a certain amount of stratification. Lenski also agreed with the conflict theorist's explanation of the uneven power of societies and the struggle that occurs because of it. He taught that political power is important but stratification is due to the distribution of surplus wealth.

Social Stratification in the United States

In the United States, class boundaries are indistinct and movement occurs frequently between classes. Americans, in general, have a very low level of class consciousness, awareness of common class interests. Americans suffer from a false consciousness in that they believe that their societal system grants them opportunity; their perception of reality is not consistent with situational reality.

The United States is highly stratified with the most visible marker of that being the unequal distribution of wealth. Income levels are astoundingly different from one class to another, and a small minority of wealthy owns the majority of all assets. Power is unequally shared as well, with the majority of power lying with the upper levels of government and corporations.
Symbols of prestige, however, are more universally shared and available as the symbols are more readily available to more of the population. In spite of the above discrepancies, the standard of living in the US is rising, the amount of the population living in poverty is declining, and the median income is rising.

There are three methods used to analyze the American class structure:

- Reputation method: Asking what members of the society view the stratification as.
- Subjective method: Asking of what class members of a society believe they are a part.
- Objective method: Ranks people based on facts like income and occupation.

The American class system has five basic strata. Some characteristics overlap, but each has its own set of specifics.

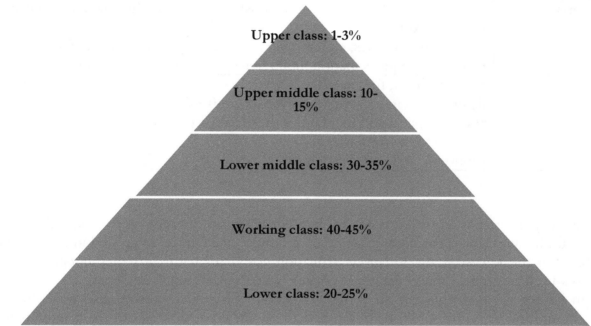

Figure 7: Five Strata of the American Class System

Class	Description
Upper class	•Very high income and wealth, college educations, high occupational prestige •Stable family •High political impact
Upper middle class	•High income, low unemployment, graduate training •Own property, affluent and comfortable lifestyle •High political participation
Lower middle class	•Few assets, some savings, modest incomes, some college •Modest standard of living •Negative attitude toward government intervention
Working class	•Low income, few to no assets, unskilled laborers, high school education, low job prestige •One-parent homes, children vocationally educated, unstable families •Little group participation, uninterested in politics, often don't vote
Lower class	•Poverty level, functional illiteracy, no interest in education, acute fiscal anxiety •Poor physical and mental health, socially isolated •Support government economic and social programs

Table 13: Description of the American Class Structure

Many social characteristics contribute to an individual's class membership. Political behavior is correlated with higher classes; the higher the strata, the more likely to be interested in politics. Divorce is more likely in the lowest strata. Religious affiliation correlates with class membership as well; the lower classes prefer evangelical and exciting services, whereas the upper classes prefer more reserved services. In higher statuses, children do better in school. The higher statuses also hold the claim to better health and longer living. Child-rearing practices are different throughout the classes as well; the higher statuses tend to guide children to adopt practices that help them shape their conduct. Lower classes tend to encourage staying out of trouble.

Poverty Concerns
Poverty can be defined in terms of relative deprivation--is a person's standard of living below that of others? In other words, is there an inability to maintain a standard of living that compares to the customary level of society? In this manner, poor is a relative terms based on a comparison with those who are not poor. Poverty can also be defined in terms of absolute deprivation. In this definition, there is an inability to provide basic sustenance.

Government social welfare programs provide benefits to the poor to help them afford the basic necessities. The benefit is determined using and annually calculated "poverty index level." In 1966, the responsibility for welfare programs shifted from the federal government to state government. Food stamp benefits were reduced, a welfare-to-work program was instituted, and child care services were promoted.

The poor is a diverse group, consisting of people who work fulltime at unskilled jobs, those who are chronically unemployed, those who live in depressed areas, and those who are underemployed. Some people are fortunate enough to climb out of poverty each year.

Poverty is often considered negatively; often the poor are thought to be lazy individuals who live off of other people's taxes. These attitudes have little bearing in reality. Sociologists argue that poverty is the result of factors outside the control of the victim.

Explanations of Poverty
Oscar Lewis discovered a <u>culture of poverty</u>, a set of values and norms common to a subculture, the poor. This culture is prevalent through urban poor regions worldwide. The telling characteristics of this culture include:

- Inability to resist impulsive gratification
- suspicious of all authority
- Lacking in a plan for the future
- Having a sense of resignation

Sociologists looked for a structural reason behind poverty in the 1970s. They sought to figure out if the unequal distribution of power, wealth, and resources caused poverty. Factors that may result in a structural reason for poverty include:

- Limited access to decent paying jobs
- Racism/persistent discrimination
- Exploiting the poor

Race and Ethnic Relations
Though racial and ethnic diversity is widespread in almost every industrial society on the globe, discrimination and inequalities still wreak havoc on social structures. Most discrimination is along racial and ethnic lines. Minority groups are those who share a biological, social, or cultural trait different from those of the majority group. The two types of traits that distinguish minority groups are:

- Culturally determined traits: dress, language, and hairstyle
- Biologically determined traits: skin color and hair texture

Ethnic groups usually share cultural traits that are passed down generationally (<u>ethnicity</u>) and racial groups share physical traits that are genetically different (<u>race</u>). While race is a social fact, sociologists explore the significance people place on that fact. Some of today's anthropologists consider race to be a cultural trait, rather than a strictly biological one. Sociologists view ethnic groups as easily distinguishable from the larger culture. Racial differences are passed down genetically while ethnic differences are learned culturally.

<u>Minority groups</u> consist of people who share physical attributes or cultural practices that are different than the main culture and this difference makes them susceptible to unusual or unequal treatment. Minority groups can be based on either race or ethnicity. There are five properties of every minority group. They are:

1. Exploited by (or suffer damages from) the dominant group.
2. Identified by at least one socially visible characteristic.
3. Share a common identity and share a strong sense of solidarity.
4. Born into the group (i.e. They are members due to an ascribed status).
5. Marry within the group (usually).

Patterns
The relationship between races and ethnicities can follow many patterns. There are three patterns of acceptance that illustrate how minorities are brought into the dominant society. And there are four patterns of rejection that explain how minorities are excluded or not accepted as part of the dominant group.

Here are the patterns of acceptance:
1. Assimilation: Ideal method of minority absorption into the dominant culture.
   - Cultural assimilation: Where the minority group loses its own distinctive cultural features and instead adopts those of the dominant group.
   - Racial assimilation: Where distinctive physical differences disappear as a result of interbreeding.
2. Amalgamation: Biologically merging racial and ethnic groups into the dominant.
3. Cultural pluralism: Retaining minority culture while also fully embracing the culture of the dominant society.

Here are the four distinct patterns of rejection:
1. Annihilation and genocide:
   - Annihilation occurs when the dominant groups causes the death of a large percentage of the minority group.
   - Genocide is a deliberate and systematic elimination of an ethnic or racial group.
2. Expulsion: Forcing a minority out of an area of society.
3. Partition: Using political boundaries to separate racial and/or ethnic groups from participating in the dominant society.
4. Segregation: Socially and legally separating ethnic and/or racial groups from the dominant society.

Perspectives

Functionalist Perspective:
Functionalists believe that any social inequality can benefit society as a whole, except when considering the impact of racial or ethnic discrimination. While behaviors such as these seem to be beneficial from the dominant society's viewpoint, in the long term, these behaviors prove to be dysfunctional.

Conflict Perspective:
Conflict theorists believe that social inequalities develop from the inherent competition between groups for resources. The most common resources fought over are: wealth, power, and prestige. Whoever wins these resources becomes (or remains) the dominant society and the others are relegated to the position of minority groups.

Racism, Prejudice, and Discrimination:
Racism is the belief that one ethnicity or racial group is inferior to another. Racism justifies unequal treatment. Institutional racism takes the form of policies that seem to be racially neutral on the surface but actually limit opportunities for minority groups. This effect is often unintentional and is commonly seen in the American economic and educational institutions. Internal colonialism is an economic exploitation in which the dominant group places minorities as subordinates for cheap labor.

Affirmative action is a set of policies that grant preferences to minorities in an effort to make up for past discrimination. This legal action began in the 1960s and is supposed to grant minorities equal access to educational and employment opportunities. These measures are highly controversial, however, because some feel they are actually a means of "reverse discrimination."

The dominant society is influenced by actions of its minority groups.

- Passive acceptance: Minorities accept the current situation.
- Aggression: Expressions of dissatisfaction, verbal, written, or physically violent.
- Collective protest: Minorities band together to express dissatisfaction.
- Self-segregation: Voluntary separation from the dominant society.
- Voluntary assimilation: Attempting to blend into the dominant society by learning the culture.

Prejudice is a rigid, irrational attitude toward a group of people based on racial or ethnic differences. Differences among group members are ignored while generalized negative feelings are present.

Sources of prejudice include:
- Stereotype: An exaggerated, and usually unfavorable, belief about a group of people. Every member of the group is assumed to have those traits.
- Authoritarian personality: Traits of a prejudiced thinker (conformity, intolerant, and

insecure).

- Irrationality: Illogical, irrational, or inconsistent beliefs about groups of people.
- Scapegoating: Projecting blame onto another person or group who is powerless to stop the threat.
- Social environment: Either encourages or discourages prejudicial behavior. Social environments that encourage prejudice include competitions, inequality, and minimal contact between members.

Discrimination is an unequal treatment, usually negative or limiting, of individuals based on their race, ethnicity, or other group membership. Prejudice does not always lead to discriminatory actions. Legal discrimination is unequal treatment that is legal. For example, workplaces hire only certain kinds of employees if hiring otherwise would hurt their image or the safety of their customers. Institutionalized discrimination refers to unequal treatment based on social custom or routine. For example, organizations exclude certain groups of individuals based on long-standing traditions and customs.

Race Relations in the United States

The relationship of different races into United States culture has historically been determined by how closely they resemble or relate to the dominant WASP (White, Anglo-Saxon, and Protestant) society. For those who were similar either racially or ethnically, the inclusion into American society was smoother. For those, however, who shared less similarity, it was a rougher amalgamation. For those even more different, both racially and ethnically, it was nearly impossible, especially at first to get a foothold into the dominant society.

The size and skill level of minority groups entering the dominant society also played a large part in how well they blended. For example, small groups of highly skilled workers were more readily accepted. Large groups of unskilled workers were seen as lazy or incompetent and avoided or shunned.

Sex and Gender Roles

There are two biologically distinctive categories of humans (sex), male and female. Gender refers to culturally learned differences between males and females and socially learned traits. Gender roles are the socially acceptable behaviors of each sex. Such gender differences are due, according to most sociologists, to both social conditioning and circumstances.

Gender inequality exists just as racial and ethnic inequality does. Different roles are unequally ranked or judged and the social statuses of the sexes continue that unequal trend.

The biological differences that actually exist between the sexes are anatomical, genetic, and hormonal. Anatomically, it is obvious what the difference is (genitalia). Genetically, females have two X chromosomes while males have an X and a Y. Both males and females produce the three main sex hormones testosterone, progesterone, and estrogen. However, each sex produces a different mix. Males produce more testosterone and females produce more estrogen.

The psychological differences between the sexes include behavior, mental ability, and personality. For example, men are usually better at math and more aggressive while women are usually more nurturing and emotional. It is hard to tell if these differences, however, are inherited or learned. Most likely, it is a combination of predisposition and environmental cues.

Sex is a constant but gender is based on societal roles. Historically, each sex has fulfilled their gender roles. Generally, this leads women into more passive and physically weak roles while men took the tough and strong roles. Gender identity is one's self-concept of being male or female. Gender roles have undergone some societal changes in the last decades. Only time will tell if any major shifts will occur in the most popular gender role assumptions.

Perspectives

Functionalist Perspective:
Functionalists opine that because gender differences have existed since the beginning of history, they must serve positively in the cohesiveness of society. When duties are assigned according to sex, an efficient means of labor division means more work is done quicker and no decisions have to be made on what to teach each new child. With this comes social stability.

Conflict Perspective:
Conflict theorists claim that gender inequality is another form of social stratification. In this form, even though women are found at every position as men are in today's society, women are viewed as inferior to men in the same standing. Because males dominate the society and because they enjoy their superiority, they are unlikely to change the status quo concerning gender inequality.

Sexism
Sexism is the belief that one sex is inferior to another and that difference justifies unequal treatment. This view is rooted in biology where many view gender differences originate. Inequalities are evident in almost every society – with men being the dominant forces. Media, language, and in some cases, religion endorse this view. Several movements and legislative measures have attempted to bridge the inequality gap.

- The feminist movement of the 1960s brought about much change and a challenge to society to break from historical molds.
- The Equal Pay Act of 1963 legislated that men and women be paid the same wage for doing the same job.
- The Equal Rights Movement of 1972 insisted that sex should not be a reason to deny someone equal rights.

Despite such measures, earnings inequalities still exist. Men still tend to have the most to gain from marriage as well. Women must maintain the home and provide care even if they pursue employment outside its walls. The wage gap still exists, though it has shrunk. Women earn about 65% of what men do in the same or relative positions. There are three commonly referred to reasons for the inequalities that exist in the workplace. They are:

- Human capital model: Men and women contribute unequally to the labor market and invest in training and education unequally. This is commonly attributed to women's lack of desire to expend more energy outside their home/families.
- Considered choice model: Women choose lower-end jobs that require less from them because of their family/home commitments.
- Discrimination model: Women are commonly placed in jobs that lack equal wages or promotion opportunity. These types of jobs are commonly called "pink-collar" jobs and consist of such placements as waitress, cashier, and receptionist.

Women are historically underrepresented in politics, even though they tend to be more politically active.

Aging

Stratification based on age revolves around how people are treated differently according to their age. In this way, age is a social status. The traditional stages of human aging include childhood, maturity, and old age. Modern stages of human aging offer more variety and include infancy, childhood, adolescence, young adulthood, middle age, old age. Age, and perceived age, is an important social status; it affects every relationship and societal expectations. Because of the importance of age, many societies have instituted rites of passage, or formal ceremonies that mark one's transition from one age status to the next. For example, graduation and retirement are two widely practiced rites of passage in the American society.

Different responsibilities and rights are established in each society based on age. For example, in pre- industrial societies, the old were highly valued for their knowledge and wisdom. In industrialized societies, however, the status of the old is very different. With the boom of technology, the old is not revered for the same reasons; their knowledge and wisdom is not necessary for the survival of the community.

Perspectives

Functionalist Perspective:
Functionalists attempt to explain the attitude that today's society has toward the elderly as one that benefits every member, including the old. Rather than having the young, middle aged, and elderly all fighting for the same roles in the labor market, the elderly are generally guided out of employment while the young are simultaneously being trained to take over.

Conflict Perspective:

Conflict theorists assert that age categories are social strata and are hierarchically ranked according to power, prestige, and wealth as the competition for social resources heats up. Everyone will belong to each age group, if they live long enough. Conflict theorists argue that due to the surplus of labor in the market, the middle-aged group has taken over and keeps the young in school (and out of the workplace) and pushes the elderly into retirement (and out of the workplace) so as to secure their own economic and social power.

Ageism

Ageism is the belief that one age strata is inferior to another and that this difference justifies unequal treatment. Ageism against the elderly is subtle, but it is pervasive. Some of the stereotypical inaccuracies that pervade an ageist's thoughts are:

- The old are not productive, or not as productive as younger people.
- Elderly people are largely infirm.
- Elderly people are senile.
- Elderly people must be confined to nursing homes (mostly because of the above reasons).

Social Gerontology

Social gerontology is the study of the social aspects of aging. This is a newer area of study simply because people are living longer now than ever before and it studies the various aspects of transitioning to old age. It examines the influence of social forces on the old and the aging process, and it also examines the societal impact of their needs.

Aging involves three processes:

- Physical aging: The body changes that accompany maturation.
- Psychological aging: Personality changes.
- Social aging: Transitions between social statuses.

Each individual experiences aging differently, and they each place different meanings to the process. Adolescence today is a much different experience than it was several decades ago. This phenomenon is discussed in the sociological concept of a cohort – a category of people born during the same time period. Each cohort views things with some similarity as other cohorts, but completely differently from cohorts of a different generation.

As people have aged and social gerontologists have observed them, four perspectives have emerged to explain how they have adjusted to aging.

- Disengagement theory: Elderly withdraw from society (and society withdraws from the elderly). Social roles diminish, leading many to depression.
- Activity theory: Elderly reduce their levels of activity and involvement due to societal structures, but if they can maintain some of their activity level, they feel better about themselves.

- Continuity theory: The elderly are simply continuing their life journey and will tend to deal with the changes at this stage similar to how they dealt with change throughout their life.
- Aged as a subculture: Elderly, feeling separate from other age groups, seek to spend their time with others of the same subculture.

The Graying of America

The post-World War II 'baby boom' phenomenon has impacted every area of American life. An unprecedented number of babies were born between 1946 and 1964. In the 1950s and 60s, the American education system had to develop in ways to handle the influx of the 76 million children born during that surge. Colleges had to soon do the same thing. Figure out how to enlarge or bust.

In the 1970s, the job market was flooded; unemployment rose. Into the 21st century now, this generation is retiring causing Americans of every age to think about Social Security and other supportive services aimed at this generation.

As age creeps up on an individual, he or she may notice their hair graying, vision loss, hearing deficits, and slow reflexes. All of these biological changes make for large adjustments to daily life. Mental functioning and agility usually impedes social interactions, leaving the aging feeling more alone than ever. Chronic medical conditions usually develop or are worsened by the body's physical aging process.

Retirement has become a reality (or forced reality) for the elderly since the Social Security Act of 1935 that made it possible for the oldest members of society to be financially free from work. As age increases, it becomes more necessary for an individual to have housing close to essential services, like health care, transportation, and food. For this reason, retirement communities are popular, but these facilities isolate the old from younger age groups. In fact, family care is the preferred method of living for the aged, but it is not monetarily feasible in most cases, resulting in even more choosing to live in communities or homes.

Today's health care system is being pressured to change in response to rising costs, new diseases, and moral issues. Socioeconomic factors tend to force some life-saving decisions. If medical insurance won't pay and the individual can't afford a potentially life-saving, but expensive, treatment, what is the ethical choice?

Chapter Review

Activity 1: Multiple-Choice
Identify the correct answer to the question.

1. The movement of an individual from one class to another over time is an example of:
   A. Upward mobility
   B. Social mobility
   C. Intergenerational mobility
   D. Downward mobility

2. Which theory generally agrees that the individuals who contribute the most to a society's success get the largest reward?
   A. Functionalism
   B. Evolution theory
   C. Conflict theory
   D. Symbolic interaction theory

3. The political dimension of Weber's stratification models, was referred to as what?
   A. Party
   B. Status
   C. Power
   D. Class

4. Classes are defined in terms of their relationship to which one of the following?
   A. Life chances
   B. Capitalism
   C. The means of production
   D. The infrastructure of society

5. Class is very obvious.
   A. True
   B. False

6. Class influences the kind of access an individual has to society's resources.
   A. True
   B. False

7. Caste systems use an ascribed status to place individuals.
   A. True
   B. False

8. There is a possibility of an individual changing his or her status in a(n):
    A. Closed system
    B. Open system
    C. Caste system
    D. Gerontological system

9. Weber theorized that class includes which element(s)?
    A. Prestige
    B. Power
    C. Wealth
    D. All of the above

10. Conformity and intolerance are the trademark traits of which one of the following?
    A. Authoritarian control
    B. Institutionalized discrimination
    C. Scapegoating
    D. Prejudicial thinking

11. How easily minority groups have become part of the American society was largely dependent on which factor?
    A. Similarity to the dominant group
    B. Historical circumstances of arrival
    C. Economic circumstances
    D. All of the above

12. Ranking high in one area of social achievement being a strong indicator of ranking high in another social achievement is the definition of which term?
    A. Social status
    B. Status consistency
    C. Status inconsistency
    D. Socioeconomic status

13. An oversimplified, often derogatory, belief about a group of people is:
    A. Salient
    B. Prejudice
    C. Stereotype
    D. Discrimination

14. Whether a person views themselves as male or female is their:
    A. Gender identity
    B. Sex
    C. Gender
    D. Hermaphroditism

15. Whether a person is biologically male or female is their:
    A. Gender identity
    B. Sex
    C. Gender
    D. Hermaphroditism

Activity 2: Short Answer
Answer the questions or prompts as fully as possible using the knowledge you have gained in this chapter.

1. Define social stratification.

2. What are the two types of stratification?

3. What is the difference between race and ethnicity?

4. What is the difference between prejudice and discrimination?

Chapter Review Answers

Activity 1:
1. B
2. A
3. C
4. C
5. B
6. A
7. A
8. B
9. D
10. D
11. D
12. B
13. C
14. A
15. B

Activity 2:
1. The term social stratification refers to the structure of inequalities across social groups.
2. The two types of stratification involve open systems, where status change is possible, and closed systems, where status change is unlikely or impossible.
3. Race relates to physical characteristics passed on genetically from generation to generation. Ethnicity refers to cultural characteristics passed on socially.
4. Prejudice is a rigid, irrational attitude, usually negative, toward a group of people. Discrimination is the unequal treatment of groups of people.

Chapter 5: Social Institutions

What's the point?

- To define "family" and explain different family patterns.
- Understand various types of marriage and the patterns of descent.
- Identify the influence of divorce, marriage, and cohabitation on the traditional American family dynamic.
- Explain the sociological importance of educational institutions, their structure, and inequalities.
- Explain the sociological importance of religious institutions, and identify their classification systems, and current trends.
- Explain power and the four types of legitimate power.
- Explain the sociological importance of health, illness, and disease and trace the development of medicine.
- Understand the basic segments of the economy, and the key terms associated with each.
- Understand how institutions develop and what needs are met by them.

Social institutions naturally occur to fill a need in the society. The institutions discussed in this chapter are found in most every society in the world. The way each operates may be different, but these institutions are necessary to meet the needs of the people.

Family

Family refers to the ancient and most basic of social institutions and is still a fundamental part of all societies. A family is a relatively permanent group of individuals who are related by ancestry, marriage, or adoption who also live together and take care of young. When a family is formed through marriage, it legitimizes the offspring of the relationship. This is still a social expectation and can take place through a religious figure who sanctions the marriage through a cultural ritual or a governmental figure who simply records the fact of the marriage.

There are two types of families. Most individuals are members of both types during the course of their life. They are:

- Family or orientation: The family an individual is born into. This offers most socialization opportunity.
- Family of procreation: The family that individuals create by marrying and having children.

Patterns

There are a variety of family patterns between cultures. There are common dimensions studied and identified as markers of patterns. They are:

- Family forms
- Courtship and marriage patterns:
    o Number of marriage partners
    o Partner preference
- Residence patterns
- Authority patterns
- Descent and inheritance patterns

Family Forms:

Traditionally, extended families have played an important role in societal makeup. An <u>extended family</u> is one that consists of more than two generations living as a unit either under one roof or in close proximity. Now, however, nuclear families (or conjugal families) is the American ideal. The nuclear family consists of a couple and their children living separately from their other family members. This nuclear family has some advantages and disadvantages as the following chart illustrates.

Advantages	Disadvantages
Geographic mobility	Smaller support structure
Social mobility	Death or prolonged illness of breadwinner can lead to crisis
Economic advantages	

Figure 8: Advantages and Disadvantages of the Nuclear Family

Multiple families of related individuals make up a wider network of relatives or kin. Kinship is a network of families who are related by common ancestry, adoption, marriage or affiliation. Cultural norms dictate the relationships and the exact membership of the kinship. While the members may not all live together, they share certain responsibilities and obligations. In modern societies, the family unit tends to become more isolated from all but the closest kin.

<u>Single-parent families</u>, families with only one parent, have emerged as a result of disease and death historically. Today, many choose to be a single parent rather than to give their child up for

adoption or marry someone they do not feel they want to share a life with. More single-parent household are evolving after divorce proceedings as well. In the case of divorced couples, the binuclear family is another family pattern that has evolved. In this case, the couple divorces and each create their own family with the child. When joint custody is ordered, both parents still share responsibility for the child(ren) equally. In this case both parents try to focus not on family disintegration, but on redefining and reorganizing their family.

The reconstituted family, also known as stepfamilies, consists of those in which one of the parents has included children from a previous marriage into their household. Blended families, also known as combined families, consist of parents and children from each of the parents' previous marriages. Death and divorce charge a high toll to today's families.

Societies also tend to differentiate between children born in wedlock (considered a legitimate birth) and those born out of wedlock (considered illegitimate births).

Courtship and Marriage Patterns:
Courtship allows potential partners to showcase or promote their assets, talents, and ambitions. Partners are generally attracted by similar characteristics like: age, social class, religion, education, goals, family plans, etc. Another stage that many couples explore before marriage is cohabitation, living together without a legal marriage.

Romantic love is unique in that it involves physical and emotional attraction. Romantic love helps to shift loyalty from the family of orientation to a family of procreation. It also offers emotional support and promotes the idea of marriage. For successful relationships, romantic love must grow into rational love (communication, giving, receiving, and accepting). Compatibility, mutual support, and social similarity are necessary for a lasting relationship.

Marriage is a social institution found in every society; it is also an economic arrangement between a man and woman that involves sexual intimacy. In this socially approved arrangement, procreation legitimizes offspring. It is most common for people to marry someone from the same social class (called endogamy). This practice, largely unconscious, maintains ethnic norms. Some cultures, however, encourage exogamy, the practice of marrying someone from a different social class. In the United States, marital choice is limitless for the most part. Homogamy is the practice of marrying someone very similar to one's self, according to race, ethnicity, social class, religion, etc., and is the choice of most Americans.

While most marriages in the world consist of one man and one woman (monogamy), there are several examples of relationships that include two or more partners. Polygamy is a form of marriage in which a person has more than one spouse simultaneously. Polygyny is when a man marries two or more women. Polyandry is when a woman marries two or more men. Polyamory is group marriage of a union between more than one man with more than one woman.

Notes on Divorce:

According to the Centers for Disease Control, the divorce rate in America is 3.5 per 1,000 total population. Currently, about 50% of marriages end in divorce. Typically, the longer a marriage lasts, the chance of divorce decreases, and most divorces occur within the first seven years.

The likelihood of a marriage ending in divorce increases if any of the following conditions apply to the relationship:

- The couple married young
- The couple married after a short courtship
- The couple lives in an urban setting
- Friends/relatives of the couple disapprove of the union
-

Divorce involves the entire family, not just the couple. Children suffer. Some of the negative impacts divorce has on children include an obviously less positive relationship with their parent(s), problems at school, and social isolation. These factors can lead to addictions and eating disorders. Children of every age have expressed anger, fear, abandonment issues, sadness, rejection, and guilt. If parents can maintain a positive relationship during a divorce and avoid conflict, children will adapt better. They will still have to adjust to one less parental figure and the stress that the family is likely to experience with less income.

Marriages suffer breakdown for several different reasons. Some of them are listed here.

- Stress on the nuclear family
- Ending of romantic love, if not followed or shifted to rational love
- Changed role of women can threaten the stability of the male's ideal
- Sexual permissiveness takes the trust of the couple and shatters it

Most divorced people tend to remarry within 3-4 years. Eight out of ten of these remarriages include children. 60-75% of remarriages fail due to several factors:

- Step-parenting problems
- Carrying over problems from first marriage into second
- Reacting quicker to signs of marital problems
- Ease of getting a divorce

Notes on Widowhood:

Death is another source of the changing face of families. Millions of men and women are widowed (mostly women). It is not unusual for widowers to be completely cut off from friends and family and to continue leading an isolated life. Widows are usually more economically troubled than widowers.

Residence Patterns
Residence patterns follow the norms of the society. There are three types of residential living pattern:

1. Patrilocal residence: Custom dictates that married partners dwell in or near the husband's father
2. Matrilocal residence: Custom dictates that married partners dwell in or near the wife's father
3. Neolocal residence: Custom dictates that married partners dwell in a new residence separate from the kin of either spouse

Authority Patterns:
Authority patterns follow the norms of society, as well, but they are also affected by the personality of each spouse. The types of marital authority are:

1. Patriarchy: Husband has more authority in the family
2. Matriarchy: Wife has more authority in the family
3. Egalitarian: Husband and wife share authority equally in the family

While patriarchy is the most common and prevailing pattern, many modern societies have adopted the egalitarian approach.

Descent and Inheritance Patterns:
Inheritance and family descent occurs in three basic ways:

1. Patrilineal system: Descent and inheritance passes through the male side of the family
2. Matrilineal system: Descent and inheritance passes through the female side of the family
3. Bilateral system: Descent and inheritance passes through both sides of the family

The Changing of American Families
The horizon of the American family has changed drastically. Now, due in part to more single-parent households, cohabitation, serial monogamy, reconstituted families, childless couples, gay couples, "open" marriages, dual career families, and more, the face of the American family is different with each passing generation. Sociologists expect the nuclear family to adjust to the changing social and economic climate as needed. Some of the key changes are discussed below.

- Demographics have played a key role in many family trends. Increased life expectancy, smaller families, children born later in life, and more women in the labor force have affected the nuclear family.
- The number of single-parent and stepfamilies has increased.
  - Single-parent families usually suffer more instability, emotional stress, and relocation along with the role changes usually inherent in a one-parent household.

- o Blended families usually deal with issues like role confusion, tension, jealousy, and insecurity. It usually takes 3-6 years to fully form a new family.
- One of the most significant social changes that have affected the family includes the entrance of women in the work force. This has changed gender roles, created 'latchkey' kids, and increased finances. Dual-income families provide a larger income for the family, but usually at the cost of a more hectic lifestyle.
- Family violence is increasing, unfortunately. It is unequally distributed among society; in spousal abuse, it is directly linked to low income. Sexual abuse occurs most often in middle and upper- middle income families. The stress related to economic distress is thought to be the central reason behind family violence. Substance abuse is another indicator.
  - o Child abuse includes physical abuse, neglect, sexual abuse, incest, and murder.
    - Statistically, teen mothers are more likely to abuse their children than are more mature mothers.
    - 70% of men who abuse their spouses also abuse their children.
    - 50% of sexual abuse is committed by relatives or friends.
    - Almost one-third of child murders occur at the hand of the mother's boyfriend.
  - o Abuse against adults includes wife battering, marital rape, husband abuse, and elderly abuse.
    - Four million women are battered each year – across all socioeconomic levels.
    - Batterers are usually male, unemployed, and have low income.
    - 5% of elderly are abused by primary caretakers.

Perspectives

Functionalist Perspective:
According to functionalists, the family is the foundation of social order. This perspective focuses on how the family meets the needs of its members and contributes to social stability. The four functions of the family, according to functionalist theory, in the modern society are:

- Socialization: Families are where children learn appropriate behavior and what is expected of them throughout life.
- Affection and companionship: Families provide the primary source of love and affection impacting children's physical, intellectual, and emotional growth.
- Sexual regulation: Families are the arena where socially acceptable sexual activity can result in legitimate children.
- Economic consideration: Families are an economic unit, either producing or consuming goods as a unit.

Conflict Perspective:
This perspective insists that the family is the principle institution of male dominance over women. Conflict theorists believe that the sexes compete with each other and that family benefits are not equally divided.
Conflict theorists also believe that capitalism was instituted as a means of keeping inequality of the sexes. Capitalism does not monetarily reward female duties of childbirth, health care, etc.).

Educational

Education is the formal vehicle for transmission of knowledge, technical skills, cultural values, and norms. Job requirements increase the need for education, and according to the U.S. Bureau of the Census, the higher a householder's income is, the greater their potential earnings are. For these reasons, education is a highly prized integral part of American society.

In the United States, education is the largest industry, even though everyone can attend free of charge. (Public school funds come from local property taxes.) Compulsory education laws are enacted in every state – for elementary, middle school, and high school levels. 82% of Americans are high school graduates and 23% are college graduates.

Structure

One major problem in the public school system is that the bureaucratic process interferes with the learning process. From the local and state level up to the federal level directives have been initiated that make it difficult for administrators and faculty to fulfill their daily obligations while complying with the mandates. Because these directives usually have money, or the qualification of money, attached to them, it is imperative that schools on a budget strive to maintain those mandates.

Another major problem with the public school system is the inequality that exists across geographic area. Schools rely on tax money and federal aid to fund programs like Head Start and school lunch programs. Certain geographic areas have a greater tax pool to pull from.

The role of teachers in the school system is varied. From disciplinarian to judge, confidante to counselor, substitute parent to colleague and employee, a teacher's day is unique. On top of those responsibilities, many parents state that they believe teachers should be held to "higher" standards than societal norms because they are impressing young minds.
Students usually fall into three subcultures:

- Academic: Intellectual leaders, high grades, academic activities
- Fun: Popular students, social, athletics/parties/dating
- Delinquent: Rebellious toward authority, rules, and/or structure

The school system encourages competition in four different ways. Competition is not necessarily a bad thing; it is integral to the socialization process.

1. Number/letter grading system: The normal means of determining whether students have grasped the information provided to them or not.
    a. It is easy, however, for students to lose track of learning, and simply learn how to make a good grade.
    b. Teachers can easily lose sight of learning verses a great record of achieving students.
2. Standardized testing: In this often debated assessment, social and racial inequalities are perpetuated by the educational facilities.
    a. SATs are used as a test for college aptitude.
3. Self-fulfilling prophecy: This includes labeling which can lead to certain academic successes and failures. Labeling someone as a 'jock' can keep them from even trying to achieve academic success. They'll lean toward fulfilling what is already said about them.
4. IQ test: As a measure of intelligence, this test may show a cultural bias in the wording of the questions and the subject matter tested.

Inequality in Schools

Even though education is free and compulsory, inequalities still exist due to poverty and social isolation. This stratification-based distribution of education preserves social inequality. It is still a fact that the class to which an individual is born strongly influences their social success or failure. Discrepancies in equality exist between social classes and races, and more pronounced between public and private schools.

Many hypothesize that if quality of teachers, funding, and materials were all representatively equal in every school district, there would be no inequality. A controversial report by James Coleman refutes this assertion. The Coleman report stated that student background and socioeconomic status is a more important indicator in determining educational outcomes than the amount of money spent per student.

Lower class children often find it harder to succeed in school, because they do not believe they can and because they are less knowledgeable about how to succeed. Children raised in poverty, in single-parent homes, and with language barriers are the most at risk of dropping out of school. De jure segregation – segregation upheld by law – was declared unconstitutional during Brown v. Board of Education. De facto segregation – segregation based on geographic area – took its place. This did not reprieve any of the inequalities that existed. It simply highlighted the differences. Children would attend the school closest to them. In poor neighborhoods, income was low and thus schools were poorly staffed.

Several options to overcome these adversities have been offered over the years to help establish success at every socioeconomic level and no matter the learning difficulty. Two such options were magnet schools and majority-to-minority transfer. Magnet schools are located in inner cities and offer special academic programs aimed at encouraging middle class, suburban students. Majority-to-minority transfer refers to a free transportation program that helps students move from a school where they are a majority to one where they are a minority. These programs are helping to diversify the racial mix within many school systems in America.

U.S. Educational Trends

For at least the last 30 years, the American school system has been attacked by several different groups whose aim is noble; their aim is to improve what they perceive to be an inadequate or inept system. Declining scores on achievement tests seem to highlight these complaints. Teachers are being charged with not meeting the most basic of educational needs. In fact, math and science skills are seriously lacking in graduating students today. Tested against 41 other countries, American students only rank in the average range.

According to the U.S. Department of Education, the top concerns expressed by citizens about the school system are:

- Lack of discipline
- Teaching quality
- Violence
- Lack of finances
- Drug use
- Overcrowding
- Low academic standards
- Weak curricula

The threat of educational decline worries most Americans so much that they are willing to fund improvements in the system through greater taxation. Some such innovations include:

- Closed circuit television used in the classroom
- Team teaching
- Open classrooms
- Paraprofessionals
- Computers (now almost universal at every level of education)

These programs have had varied success. Voucher systems have also been instituted that have given families a choice of where to send their children to school, whether it be a private, charter, or magnet school.

Perspectives

Functionalist Perspective:

From a functionalist perspective, education provides many intended, and some unintended, functions and is necessary for social function. An unintended function of education is childcare. The five intended functions of education include:

1. Socialization: The culturally-based transmission of knowledge, technical skills, values, and norms.
   a. Geography, math, science, communication along with politics, behavior, morality, and heritage.
2. Social control: Teaching culturally appropriate behavior, cooperation, loyalty, and obedience.
3. Selection and allocation: Screening and selection for different types of jobs through diplomas and certifications.
4. Assimilation: Social integration of minorities into the dominant society through the teaching of the English language, patriotism, U.S. history, customs, and traditions.
5. Innovation and change: Develops new knowledge and skills to add to the cultural heritage. Education stimulates intellectual curiosity and provides opportunity for research and experimentation.
   a. Basic research: Systematic inquiry concerned with establishing new knowledge by uncovering basic aspects.
   b. Applied research: experimenting with practical uses of existing knowledge.

Conflict Perspective:

In direct contrast, the conflict theorist believes that the educational system is the vehicle that perpetuates social inequalities. School is an important aspect of moving from one social status to another, but the relationship between a parent's social status and their child's educational success is direct. Social programs tend to use educational programs in an attempt to gain or maintain power, wealth, or prestige. In fact, the ruling class uses two powerful tools to limit access to higher educational opportunities. These tools are:

- Tracking: Grouping students into classes based on standardized tests. In this system, students are grouped together in an effort to direct them toward specialized goals. Dividing children in the 'smart' and 'not smart' leads to a self-fulfilling prophecy.
- Credentialism: Asking for specific advanced degrees even though the knowledge obtained by those degrees does not in any way correlate to their work tasks.

Religious

Religion is a system of beliefs and practices by which a group of people interpret and react to what they feel is sacred. Evident in every society, religion is universal, and yet it is diverse. Almost every religion in the world requires faith. Four more common elements present in most religions are:

- Sacred objects or places: such as an altar, cathedral, or burial mound.
- Rituals: Formalized procedure or behavior
- Beliefs: Defines and establishes protection for the sacred and relates the sacred objects to the rituals.

- Believers: Those who conduct the rituals, care for the sacred, and build places of worship.

Emile Durkheim was the first sociologist to realize the importance of religion in human societies. He believed that the distinction between the 'sacred' and the 'profane' was a key differentiation in every religion. The sacred was anything deemed holy or divine as part of the supernatural. The profane was anything ordinary or routine that was often taken for granted in daily living.

Belief systems usually provide moral philosophy to its believers. It can also translate those beliefs into educational and political doctrine. An organization of believers is absolutely necessary to assure religious continuity, for ritual conduct, to proselytize, and to build places of worship. Belief systems provide coping mechanisms and other positives, including:

- Support: To overcome fear of the unknown, anxiety about the future, and hope in the case of a death.
- Understanding: Concerning the larger scheme or plan. Used as a means to judge the 'righteousness' of goals, ideals, and actions.
- Fulfillment: of a desire to have a sacred relationship, or something more than our normal or boring existence.
- Membership: that encourages the mutual sharing of sacred values and beliefs.
- Assistance: to deal with the major transitions of life, including birth, puberty, marriage, and death.

Types
Sociologists have examined the different belief systems of the world and have categorized them into four broad categories:

- Animatism: Belief system based on the existence of a spirit or force found within people, animals, plants, or inanimate objects and which contains personality and will, but no soul.
- Animism: Belief system based on the existence of a spirit or force found in everything within nature and which contains a soul.
- Theism: Belief system based on one or more supreme beings or gods who deserve to be worshipped because of their power and influence.
  - Monotheism: Belief system based on the existence of one supreme god.
  - Polytheism: Belief system based on the existence of more than one god.
- Ethical religions: Belief system based on philosophical ideals and how to achieve them.

Organizations
Religious organizations are in a process of continual change and adaptation. One denomination offshoots into another and one changes its face to focus on a different aspect of their religious beliefs. Change is constant. Sociologists have identified four types of religious organizations.

- Ecclesia: Large, formally organized religious body that is considered the national or official religion. All members of a society belong to this body. An ecclesia welds influence over the government. Ecclesias are not common today, but some organizations roughly approximate them.

- Denomination: Also known as a church, it is a well-established and socially accepted religious organization. Believers fall into the hierarchy and conform to doctrines and rituals. Denominations are usually tolerant of each other and are not officially linked to state or government.
- Sect: Sects are small and less formally organized. They have split from a denomination and in some way protest against the parent religion. They are generally uncompromising and indifferent or hostile toward government.
- Cult: Loosely organized religious movement with ideas that are in direct opposition to established and accepted religious traditions.

Perspectives

Functionalist Perspective:

Functionalists view religion as a means of integrating society members into the status quo by providing social support and reinforcement of values and norms. Religions also improve the community's solidarity and are a means of transmitting cultural heritage from generation to generation.

Conflict Perspective:

Just as they do all other aspects of society, conflict theorists view religion as a servant of the ruling class. Much of this perspective is derived from Marx's theories of social inequality. He viewed religion as a tool to keep the oppressed oblivious to their plight while they concentrated on their religious totems, rituals, and beliefs. Marx also posited that social change was averted because believers accepted social inequalities as a part of their beliefs.

U.S. Religions

Religion in America has several distinct qualities; peace of mind, security, and positively-rewarded life-after-death are emphasized. The qualities of American religion have been molded by the values of optimism and tolerance and the cultural diversity that defines the nation.

- There is no official state religion of the United States. The Constitution forbids such.
- There is a protected freedom of religion.
- Almost 70% of Americans belong to some kind of religious organization.
- The cultural assumption implicitly expects a belief in God and/or religious principles.
- Religious diversity and cultural pluralism has led to more than 75 large, organized religions.
- Tolerance toward religious diversity is evident throughout society.

- Sects and cults not tolerated.
- Religion used not only as a source of beliefs and rituals, but also as a source of identity.
- Political and social attitudes correlate with an individual's religious affiliation.

According to the most recent data available, the following table lists the top 5 religious bodies in the United States.

Religious Body	Membership
Catholic	6,640,710
Southern Baptist	1,640,000
United Methodist Church	825,104
Church of Jesus Christ of Latter-day	559,917
Evangelical Lutheran Church in America	498,492

Figure 9: Top 5 Religious Bodies in America

In general, older Americans are the most likely to be a member of a particular religion. Social statuses are sometimes given to certain religions. Often, geography plays a part in what religion people are affiliated with. Religious participation, or the actual attendance and participation in activities, is declining as more Americans find it unnecessary to attend services to be a good Christian or Jew.

Religiosity, the nature and level of personal religious experiences, is hard to evaluate as every member has differing levels of commitment. Glock identified four dimensions of religiosity:

- Experiential: The degree of emotional attachment to the supernatural
- Ritualistic: The level of participation and attendance
- Ideological: The commitment to the group's beliefs
- Consequential: The affect the religious involvement has on behavior.

Thomas Luckman suggested one more dimension of religiosity:

- Invisible religion: The idea that public service or attendance is not required because deeply held religious convictions are private.

Despite the evidence that suggests membership and participation has decreased dramatically, an increasingly emergent religious consciousness has grown in the US. Fundamentalist, evangelical organizations have grown rapidly in the last 25-30 years fostered along by television. In these religions, being "born again" and believing in the literal interpretation of the Bible is encouraged. Fundamentalists groups and right-wing politicians have similar beliefs; therefore, these groups have been influential.

Peter Berger, however, argues for the reality of secularization, the process of religion losing its influence on society. He states that perhaps religion is no longer the force that unites societies or impacts education or politics as it once did. Secularization can be registered and measured in many ways. In the modern society that is highly diversified, traditional religions can become more separate and its influence can wane (especially because other institutions, like government or science, take its place). When this happens, however, newer religions or sects develop. In reality, it is highly unlikely that a completely secularized society will ever exist. Religion answers questions that people want answered.

Political

Politics is the social process by which people and groups acquire, exercise, maintain, and/or lose power over others. It is an inevitable part of social living. Political processes, as a universal part of highly structured governments, grant rights and freedoms to citizens, assign responsibilities, and control access to and use of resources. Each political institute varies in personality according to the people who make up the group. Political order is the institutionalized system from which individuals or groups exert power over others. Power is generally channeled through political institutions, enduring social arrangements that distribute and exercise power, according to the political order of the nation.

Power is defined as the ability to control or influence the actions and behaviors of others, with or without their consent. Usually power is given to a position, not necessarily the person in that position. There are three means used to control the actions of others:

- Reward: Offering a benefit or something positive in exchange for obedience or compliance
- Punishment: Threatening or creating negative consequences for disobedience
- Influence: Manipulating information, attitudes, and feelings

Max Weber asserted that the state is the only authority able to hold supreme power in a geographic territory. This power can be delegated to certain authorities, but in the end the state can override all other agencies and is central to the political order. He also stated that power can be either:

- Illegitimate: Few in society view the people who are acting in power do not have a right to do so. Coercion is forcing a person to obey someone who is exerting illegitimate power (a bank robber, for example).
- Legitimate: Society views the power or authority to be valid and/or justified. Authority is legitimate power (a police officer, for example).

In his research and theorizing, Weber identified three types of legitimate authority. Each type is based on implicit or explicit consent of those who are under that power. All three of these types are present in most societies.

1. Traditional: Power is based on socially accepted customs and practices. It has historical roots and is religiously sanctioned; for these reasons, it is usually hereditary and an ascribed status. Leadership quality is not a requirement; people will obey because they always have.
2. Rational-legal: Power is based on rules, regulations, and procedures that are expressly designed to establish power and how it is exercised and distributed. It is based more on the position and not the person holding the position.
3. Charismatic: Power is based on the qualities of the leader, like being able to excite and inspire his/her followers. It is often unstable as it rests with the charisma of one person. This kind of leader can have a positive or negative influence on societies.

Distribution of Power

There are three perspectives concerning the distribution of political power.

1. Pluralist: Social order is achieved when the state effectively mediates interest groups, seeks public consensus and passes laws and regulations to reflect that consensus. In this perspective, the political system is a continuous bargaining process with give-and-take between all interest groups.
2. Elitist: Democracies in the modern world are led by a very small minority (the elite). Three of the leading classic elitists are Michels, Mosca, and Pareto. In this perspective, the general population is viewed as apathetic, incompetent, and unwilling or unable to govern themselves. Even in large bureaucracies, small, elite, powerful groups (oligarchies) take the lead. Modern elitists view the population as able to rule themselves but manipulated and/or exploited by the elite.
3. Class conflict: Derived from Karl Marx's works, this perspective believes that power is in the hands of a small ruling class. Conflicts are inevitable as oppressed groups attempt to overthrow the ruling class.

Types of Government

Government is classified according to the type of relationship between the ruler and the ruled and whether the government answers to the people or vice versa. The three most common types of government found throughout the world are:

- Authoritarianism: Form of government where rulers rarely consider what the public wants. Elections do not exist; civil rights are not protected. Political parties are non-existent and ideologies are not allowed. Rulers do not tolerate opposition.
- Totalitarianism: Form of government where rulers don't recognize any limits to their authority. This is an extreme form of authoritarianism that stretches to regulate all aspects of social life. Any opposition is suppressed, religious groups are persecuted, and censorship is liberal.
- Democracy: Form of government based on participation of the population; ultimate authority is vest in the people. In this type of government, decision are based on the "majority rule," and participating in government is considered a right of every citizen.

There are three main types of democracy:

1. True: All citizens have direct participation in government.
2. Representative: Citizens can vote for leaders to represent them in government. There is no guarantee that those representatives will act as their constituents would want.
3. Liberal: Supports the protections of individual rights.

Political Process

Political participation by every citizen in the political process is believed to make people more tolerant, better informed, and better equipped to self-govern. Many believe that political participation by all is detrimental to societal health as people are generally uninformed and untrained which leads them to support governmental projects which lead only to an overburdened government.

Political activity has been decreasing over the last decades. Voting, the least demanding activity, has seen this decrease as well. The exact reason is unknown, but it is probably an amalgamation of several reasons like registration processes that are more complex, gender, age, frequency of elections, etc.) Three types of such political activity are:

1. Gladiatorial: Those who hold office, campaign actively, and in other ways have a high-level of involvement.
2. Transitional: Those who attend meetings and contact officials.
3. Spectator: Those who have little involvement, perhaps voting and displaying a bumper sticker.

Political parties are organizations made up of people with similar beliefs whose aim is to gain legitimate control over government. In democracy, political parties play an important role, as they connect voters to government and illustrate alternative policy options. As votes come in, they also symbolize public opinion on a number of issues. Political parties also recruit and offer candidates for public office.

Interest Groups seek to influence government policies and public opinion. These groups can be small, large, temporary, or permanent. They all have the same goal, however, which is to gain access to those in power and influence those who vote. Many large interest groups use lobbying, a tactic that refers to attempting to persuade a decision-maker. Lobbyists are the voice of these groups.

There are several types of special interest groups.

- Public interest groups: Their goal is to represent the public good.
- Single-issue groups: They concentrate on one narrowly defined interest.
- Industry groups: Their goal is to represent large organizations.
- Political Action Committees (PACs): They aim to garner political influence by making

political contributions.

Perspectives

Functionalist Perspective:
A functionalist believes that the state emerged as a means to meet the needs of maintaining the social system/social order. The important functions of the state are as follows, according to functionalist theory:

- The state enforces norms through laws.
  - Offenders are negatively sanctioned.
- The state provides conflict resolution.
  - Policies are enacted to do just that and the state acts as arbitrator.
- The state attempts to conquer problems by providing directions and planning.
- The state works to develop important and lucrative relationships with other societies.

Conflict Perspective:
Similar to the conflict perspective in every other area, in politics, conflict theorists proclaim that the state exists to ensure the interests of the ruling class. Again, as Marx states, all societies, except the most primitive, are made up of two classes – the powerful and the exploited. Various groups use the political process to gain power. Usually, the wealthier group wins, but an ongoing conflict can eventually result in a change or shift in the distribution of power.

Models

In the pluralist model of politics, several competing interest groups have access to government and have a part in shaping its direction. Sociologists tend to point to the diversity of these groups, rejecting Mills' view of power concentration (see next paragraph).
In the power-elite model of politics, power is held by and exercised by a few. The U.S., according to C. Wright Mills, is ruled by such a small group. The positions these few hold in government, bureaucracy, big corporations, and the military, have given them influence.

Medical

Because of the universal problem of illness, a social institution (medicine) has evolved to help individuals maintain health and fight disease. In some preindustrial societies, medicine is considered an aspect of religion, with the healer being a priest or witch doctor.

Health vs. Disease

Cultural definitions of health and sickness tend to vary based on a country's level of wealth, technology, and its ability to meet the population's needs. Sociologists view <u>health</u> as the absence of disease and the ability to respond effectively to the environment. An <u>illness</u> is psychological in nature in that it is a condition where an individual perceives that he/she is suffering a bodily disorder. A <u>sickness</u> is sociological in nature in that it is a condition where others observe that an individual is suffering a bodily disease. A <u>disease</u> is biological in nature in that is a condition that is objectively diagnosed by a medical practitioner.

<u>Epidemiology</u> is the study of the origin, distribution, and transmission of a disease in the population. Discovering how a disease is transmitted helps to identify ways of preventing or eliminating the disease. Diseases can disrupt not only families and relationships, but entire societies. Different types of disease are as follows:

- Endemic: A disease that is always present in a population.
- Epidemic: A usually uncommon disease that becomes a rapidly wide-spreading outbreak that affects a significant portion of the population.
- Pandemic: A disease that has spread worldwide.
- Acute: A disease that onsets rapidly and has a short duration.
- Chronic: A disease that onsets slowly and has a long duration.

Development of Medicine

Medicine has evolved from theories of how diseases operate into treatments to effectively combat them. Louis Pasteur's Germ Theory was a turning point in the development of medicine. It switched the focus from treating the sick to understanding the disease. Pasteur surmised that most diseases are caused by microscopic organisms (germs) that enter the human body.

Medicine has grown from that first understanding to the empire that it is today. Now, an increasing number of conditions or problems are being defined as diseases and treated medically. This medicalization of society has four tenets:

- The medical institution has grown. (This is obvious)
- Life events are considered a medical condition. (Example: pregnancy)
- Deviant behavior is considered a medical condition. (Example: alcoholism)
- The public accepts the medicalization.

Perspectives

Functionalist Perspective:
Talcott Parsons, one of the first functionalists to illustrate the social role of sickness, purported that sickness is a type of deviance. The sick are exempt from social responsibilities, however, and society must pick up those roles to function properly.

Functionalists relay that the purposes of medicine in a society are:

- To maintain health in the society
- To treat disease
- To conduct research and create treatments
- To maintain social order by establishing who is sick and who isn't

Conflict Perspective:

According to conflict theorists, good health is a highly valued resource, and like all resources, it is unequally distributed in a society. Differences in quality of health and access to health care tend to fall along socioeconomic lines. Those who are wealthier and can afford better health care and are generally better educated and able to discern health problems at earlier stages.

Economic

Society needs food and shelter for survival. Economic institutions have emerged from those needs. The economy is a reference to the system for producing, distributing, and consuming goods and services in a society. Many sociologists feel that this is the most important of the five social institutions (religion, government, education, family, and economy). Economic systems sometimes define government and religious systems. Changes in the economic system affect other systems.

Every economy consists of three sectors:

1. Primary sector: This sector is largely agricultural and involves extracting resources from the environment. This includes hunting, gathering, farming and mining – all activities where individuals are directly involved in the process. Preindustrial societies are usually engaged in the primary sector.
2. Secondary sector: This sector concentrates on converting raw materials into manufactured goods. These jobs are primarily blue collar jobs. Industrial societies are engaged in this secondary sector.
3. Tertiary sector: This sector produces services like teaching, medicine, and counseling. Postindustrial societies are engaged in these service jobs.

As an economy evolves, its focus progresses from primary to secondary to tertiary, causing shifts in the dynamics of the society as a whole.

Systems

There are three basic economic systems in the world: capitalism, socialism, and mixed economies. Capitalism and socialism represent ideals that are not really met in the real world. In actuality there are societies that are mostly capitalist, those that are in the middle, and those that are mostly socialist. The types of governments found in countries with each type of economic system vary widely.

The primary concept under dispute between capitalism and socialism is property. <u>Property</u> relates to the set of rights an owner has verses those of others who do not own it. <u>Community ownership</u> means that the entire community owns the property and any member can use it. <u>Private ownership</u> means that a specific person(s) own the property. <u>Public ownership</u> means that the state or political authority owns the property on behalf of the population. Property rights are so important because those who own the means of producing goods have power over those who do not. This is the primary argument between capitalists and socialists. Capitalists argue that the best interests of all are served if public ownership is kept at a minimum. Socialists argue that private ownership results in exploitation.

Capitalism:

<u>Capitalism</u> is an economic system in which the means of production are privately owned and distributed competitively in the hopes of making a profit. In a capitalist society, it is expected that owners will attempt to make a profit. It is also assumed that supply and demand will dictate what is produced and for how much. Capitalism rests on the tenets that competition will keep prices reasonable and will put out of business those producers who are ineffective.

The three key elements of capitalism, then, are:

1. Private property ownership
2. Profit
3. Competition

The drawbacks of capitalism are:

- Inflation (increasing cost of goods and services)
- Social inequality (those who own and those who do not)
- Large poverty class (those who have can succeed, but possibly not those who don't)
- Unemployment (a continual need)
- Stagflation (unemployment combined with inflation)

Socialism:

An alternative to capitalism, <u>socialism</u> is based on Karl Marx's writings. It is an economic system in which the means of production are controlled and distributed by the state. Prices are set by the government for goods and services. A socialist economy aims to efficiently produce needed goods and services and achieve social equality by preventing individual wealth.

The central reasoning behind socialism is the belief that no one should become rich if someone else must do without necessities. Therefore, the most important priority of socialism is to meet the basic needs of the entire population.

Mixed Economies:
A mixed economy uses the central elements of free enterprise (from capitalism) with state-operated services (from socialism). The aim is to control unrestrained capitalism and provide for some distribution of goods and services on the basis of "right" rather than ability to afford. These systems are sometimes referred to as democratic socialism.

Sociology of Work
Working offers people an opportunity to add meaning to one's life. They can achieve a sense of mastery and a belief that they have something to offer society. There are many types of jobs.

- Blue-collar occupations are those involving manual labor or factory work.
- White-collar occupations are those involving office or non-manual work.
- Pink-collar occupations are those that are usually reserved for females.

The labor market is a means of connecting potential workers with employers. The primary labor market includes high-paying, prestigious occupations with extensive benefits. The secondary labor market includes low-skill occupations with low pay and few benefits.

In times of economic hardship, many blue-collar workers in the secondary labor market lose their jobs. Women, non-whites, older workers and migrant/seasonal workers have a higher percentage chance of becoming unemployed. Unemployment rates in America have been connected to oil prices, recession and recovery, and an influx of women and young workers into the labor markets.

Division of labor refers to the way work is divided between individuals and groups who are specialized in particular activities. Every society employs division of labor. Preindustrial societies have simpler division while post-industrial have the most complex divisions because of the variety of jobs needing specialization. Emile Durkheim asserted that specialization actually changes or loosens the bonds holding a society together because it encourages individualism and not community.

The term used to describe the extent members of a society are bound together is social solidarity. Social solidarity depends on the level of the division of labor. Mechanical solidarity focuses on the similarity of members in small societies where everyone does similar work. The similar work maintains the cohesion of the group. There is little individualism in these societies; they are loyal and concerned for the group. Organic solidarity is caused by a complex division of labor that leaves members interdependent. This is most common in modern societies that require complex divisions of labor. Solidarity here focuses on differences, not similarities.

The opposite of solidarity is alienation. Workers can develop a sense of alienation if they feel powerless (unable to control or influence the job), meaningless (lacking a sense of purpose), isolated (disconnected from others), and/or self-estranged (when judgments and creativity are stifled). Worker alienation can lead to high absenteeism, low self-esteem, sabotage, high turnover, or low morale.

Thankfully, the majority of American workers express satisfaction in their jobs than alienation. Researchers have identified eight factors that lead to worker satisfaction:

- Prestigious jobs that lead to personal satisfaction
- Challenging jobs that have both variety and autonomy
- Considerate supervision
- Peer interaction
- Good working conditions
- High wages
- Job security
- Advancement opportunities

To ensure worker satisfaction, some reforms have been instituted to aid in worker success. Those include:

- Job enlargement: Attempts to overcome routine and fragmented job tasks by adding tasks and variety.
- Job enrichment: Adds more tasks along with authority to allow workers the opportunity to use their own discretion, initiative, and creativity.
- Autonomous work groups: Allows a small group to complete an entire set of tasks for a project by rotating jobs and participating in the job functions of recruiting, training, evaluating, and quality control.

American Trends
There are four major trends in the American workforce. They are:

- Women in the labor market: Has been increasing since World War II. Improved gender equality, more single-parent households, and more career opportunities account for this increase.
- Deindustrialization: The movement of blue-collar manufacturing jobs from the US as they are outsourced to other nations.
- Service sector jobs: Helping to offset the decrease in manufacturing jobs, service jobs now outnumber them.
- Flexible work systems: Needed to manufacture specialized, high-quality goods; it requires workers to be or become experts in several fields.

Perspectives

Functionalist Perspective:
For the functionalist, work is a necessary part of society. It integrates individuals and provides meaningful social roles that help establish identities and meet needs. A strong economy

contributes to the overall health of the society and it affects the other interdependent institutions. Economic problems like recessions and unemployment are dysfunctional and negatively impact the entire society.

Conflict Perspective:

Conflict theorists focus on social inequality, social stratification, and employee alienation. They believe that most economic systems, and especially capitalism, are driven by power, greed, and the exploitation of the weak for the benefit of the powerful.

Chapter Review

Activity 1: Multiple Choice
Identify the correct answer to the question.

1. When a man or woman has multiple marriage partners, it is called what?
   A. Polygamy
   B. Polygyny
   C. Polyandry
   D. Monogamy

2. When a man has more than one wife, it is called what?
   A. Endogamous marriage
   B. Monogamy
   C. Polyandry
   D. Polygyny

3. Which perspective views families as a way to teach values that benefit the dominant social institutions?
   A. Symbolic interactionist
   B. Feminist
   C. Functional
   D. Conflict

4. Institutionalized systems of symbols, beliefs, and values that are practiced in a structured way by a group of people who interpret and respond to what they feel is sacred is a:
   A. Totem
   B. Secular ideology
   C. Religion
   D. Religiosity

5. What is worshipped in polytheism?
   A. A single god
   B. More than on god
   C. The profane
   D. Totems

6. Karl Marx referred to religion as:
   A. A means to reaffirm the social bonds between people.
   B. An ideology that supports the ideas of the ruling class
   C. A process by which people become religious
   D. A means to allow groups to express their spiritual convictions.

7. What is a secondary network of people that is usually related by common ancestry, adoption, marriage, or affiliation?
   A. Kinship
   B. Family
   C. Cohabitors
   D. Relatives

8. The religious organization that has broken from an established church is known as:
   A. A sect
   B. A new church
   C. A subreligion
   D. A cult

9. Forcing applicants to have certain educational credentials even if those credentials do not positively affect the ability to perform the intended job is known as:
   A. Expectancy effect
   B. Self-fulfilling prophecy
   C. Credentialism
   D. Hidden curriculum

10. Which theory asserts that the education system instills values that every citizen should know and understand?
    A. Evolutionary
    B. Conflict
    C. Functionalism
    D. Symbolic interaction

11. What is the term used for authority that originates with rules and regulations that have been codified into laws, procedure, or codes of conduct?
    A. Rational authority
    B. Rational-legal authority
    C. Charismatic authority
    D. Traditional authority

12. Power that is gained through force against the will of others is called _____.
    A. Coercive power
    B. Authoritarian power
    C. Lawless power
    D. Legitimate power

13. Which system is concerned with the production, distribution, and consumption of goods and services by a society?
    A. Political
    B. Industrial
    C. Global
    D. Economic

14. If a worker feels powerless and separated from society, he is feeling:
    A. Collectively conscious
    B. Alienation
    C. Xenophobic
    D. Anomie

Activity 2: Short Answer
Answer the questions or prompts as fully as possible using the knowledge you have gained in this chapter.

1. What are the common characteristics of the family?

2. What are the causes of marital breakdown according to the text?

3. What are the characteristics of an American education?

4. What is self-fulfilling prophecy and how is it manifested in American schools?

5. What are the basic types of religious organizations?

6. What are the three different types of authority as Weber described?

7. What are the most significant forms of government in the modern world?

8. List the five classifications of disease.

9. List the forms property ownership can take.

Chapter Review Answers

Activity 1:
1. A
2. D
3. D
4. C
5. B
6. B
7. A
8. A
9. C
10. C
11. B
12. A
13. D
14. B

Activity 2:
1. A family is a group of individuals who are related in some way, live together for a significant amount of time, care for offspring, and form an economic unit.
2. Marriage breaks down because of stress, the end of romantic love, the changing role of women, and sexual permissiveness.
3. In the American educational system, free elementary, middle, and high school education is available. It is also considered to be a tool to solve social problems.
4. Self-fulfilling prophecy is making a prediction and acting as if that prediction were already true; such actions produce the predicted results. Treating a child as a failure is an example.
5. Ecclesia, denomination, sect, and cult are the four types of religious organization.
6. Max Weber identified three types of authority – traditional, legal- rational, and charismatic.
7. The most significant forms of government in the modern world are authoritarian, totalitarian, and democratic.
8. The five classifications of disease are: endemic, epidemic, pandemic, acute, chronic.
9. Ownership can be community, private, or public.

Chapter 6: Social Patterns

What's the point?

- Understand the variables sociologists study when examining demography.
- Define urbanization, metropolis, suburb, megalopolis, and over urbanization.
- Comprehend social growth theories.
- Define "human ecology."

The population of the world is ever increasing. Limited resources make this a pressing social concern, especially in urban areas where most growth has occurred.

Demographics

Demography is the study of population. Because population affects social structure and social factors affect population size, demography has become an important avenue of sociological study. Demographers rely heavily on vital statistics, official records of births, deaths, marriages, and divorces. There are three variables that are used when examining the size, growth, and characteristics of populations. They are:

- Birth rate: The number of births per 1,000 women in a population per year. This is affected by two types of factors:
    - Biological factors: the number of women actually of childbearing age and the health of those women.
    - Social factors: the type of birth control methods available in the society.
      Age-specific birth rate refers to the number of birth per 1,000 women of a specific age range. Birth rates provide information on the fertility, the number of children the average woman is bearing, of a society. Fertility can be constrained by social factors such as abortion and infanticide. Fecundity is the potential number of children that can be born to a woman of childbearing age (20-25 babies). Fertility levels do not reach fecundity levels for various reasons including social, cultural, economic, and health reasons.

- Death rate: The number of deaths per 1,000 members of the population per year. The death rate, or mortality, of a society varies by social class.
    - Age-specific death rate refers to the number of deaths per 1,000 members of the population per year in a specific age range. One such age-specific rate is the

neonatal mortality rate, the number of deaths per 1,000 infants under one month old. Infant mortality rates refer to deaths per 1,000 children under one year old; it is the most commonly referenced number. Infant death statistics are a good indicator of a society's overall health and level of medical care.

Related to death rate statistics, life expectancy is the number of years a population's newborn is expected to live. In the United States, life expectancy is about 75 years old. Life span differs in that it is the maximum possible number of years a species can live. Life span generally stays the same for each species, while life expectancy can vary dramatically, increasing as medical intervention improves.

- Migration: The movement of people from one place to another, into or out of a society. There are two types of migration:

    o International migration: Movement from one country to another.
    o Internal migration: Movement within a country.
    o Migration rate: The difference in the number of people moving in and out of a country per 1,000 members of population. Immigrants are people who move into a country. Emigrants are those who move out of a country. Migration rates do not affect global population, but can play a significant role on affected societies. Migration is influenced by two types of factors:
        - Push factors: Reasons that push people out of a country or region, like overpopulation, horrid climate, and inadequate housing and/or employment opportunities.
        - Pull factors: Reasons that attract people to a country or region, like political or religious freedoms, pleasant weather, employment opportunities, etc.

Population composition refers to the characteristics of a population, the number and type of people. Characteristics include sex, age, race, ethnicity, household size, occupation, income, and marital status. Sociologists are primarily concerned with age and sex because those numbers impact fertility, death rates, employment, and dependents. Sex ratios are commonly plotted on simple line graphs to show the distribution of males and females at each age range in a society. In the U.S., there are more male births than female, but males have a higher mortality rate than females. Therefore, women outnumber men as they age. Of course, these ratios vary greatly by region.

The population growth rate is the difference between the number of people added to a population and the number of people subtracted from a population and expressed as an annual percentage (the difference between the number of births and the number of deaths). In general, it is the poorest countries in the world that have the largest problem with rapid population growth. In these countries, overpopulation is a real concern as food, living space, and natural resources are incapable of supporting a large population, leading to malnutrition and disease.

Demographically, there are two main categories of countries, and one intermediate category:

- Developed: Low birth rates, relatively
- Less developed: High birth and growth rates, relatively
- Intermediate: Intermediate birth and growth rates; smaller & more industrialized countries.

Theories

Malthusian Theory:
Thomas Malthus was the first to develop a theory concerning the consequences of population growth. In his theory, he posited that population tends to increase exponentially. The most critical concern in population growth is food supply. He cautioned that a population larger than the food supply can support will erupt into social chaos. The flaw in Malthusian theory is that it does not take into consideration technological advances in birth control or agriculture.

Demographic Transition Theory:
In this theory, sociologists insist that populations tend to stabilize after a certain level of economic development is achieved. Three stages of development are associated with this theory:

1. High birth rate & high death rate: In traditional societies, large numbers of children are born, but medical care is insufficient, resulting in high death rate as well, especially in infants. Populations tend to remain stabilized during this stage.
2. High birth rate & low death rate: In developing societies, the birth rate remains high, but improvements in medicine force the death rate to drop. Rapid population growth occurs.
3. Low birth rate & low death rate: In advanced industrial and emerging postindustrial societies, birth rate drops as the desire for large families diminishes (and is seen as a liability). The death rate remains low due to medical advancement. Populations become stable once again.

Rural/Urban Patterns

In America, life revolves around cities. They are the centers of finance, industry, and government. Thousands of years ago, the first towns developed around agricultural production and trade zones. Cities emerged and the social process of urbanization emerged. Urbanization is the movement of the masses from rural areas to urban areas. In the mid-nineteenth century America, rapid urbanization took place and continued until the 1960s. This trend in the modern age has drastically changed the way the last few generations have lived. In developing countries, when the population explodes, overurbanization can occur (a condition where population exceeds the ability of the society's resources).

Historically, cities were small, but industrialization prodded the growth of cities. In less developed societies, cities have a very affluent center and are surrounded by slums. In industrialized societies, a central city is surrounded by several suburbs. This economic and geographic entity of city center and suburbs is called a metropolis. A suburb is a residential area on the outskirts of a central city that enables the expansion of the urban lifestyle into previously rural areas. A megalopolis is two or more major metropolitan areas that are linked either politically, economically, socially, or geographically.

The process of urbanization follows specific patterns. Environmental and social factors interplay to form cities. Urbanism is the study of cultural and social characteristics of cities. As observations were made, several points were identified as the results of the shift from small town to urban city. They are as follows:

- Organizations grow larger and more bureaucratic
- Relationships fragment
- Business and/or government takes control of functions that were previously done at home
- Communities become interrelated and no longer self-sufficient
- Media causes the urban culture to dominate the rural cultures

Views

Classical sociologists viewed urban life pessimistically. It was thought to strain human relationships. Ferdinand Tonnies was the first to explore the differences between rural and urban living. In his theoretical continuum, there were two distinct sectors:

- Gemeinschaft: A small population where there existed a simple division of labor and most people knew each other.
- Gesellischaft: A large population where there is loose associations and a complex division of labor.

Louis Wirth examined how city life affects a person's emotions, thoughts, and interactions. Wirth noticed three specific characteristics that led to this difference:

- Size: Leaves individuals feeling lost and anonymous
- Population density: Forces individuals into specific interactions (not whole relationships)
- Social diversity: Opens individuals to different viewpoints and cultures

Modern sociologists have less pessimistic views of society. Some now view the urban environment as one ripe with opportunity. Herbert Gans painted the city as a mosaic of cultures and neighborhoods to explore and experience.

Ernest Burgess developed the <u>concentric zone model</u> that stated that cities grow outward in a series of concentric circles radiating out from the central business district. Moving away from the central core of the city is viewed as upward mobility.

Urban/Rural Comparisons

Research is not conclusive, but certain generalizations seem to be supported. For examples, urban areas tend to have higher crime rates than non-urban communities. The institution of the family is weaker in urban areas, and those living in cities tend to have fewer friends — even though they are surrounded by more people on a daily basis. City-dwellers are considered less helpful and more inconsiderate to strangers than rural-dwellers. They also tend to show less contentment with their surroundings.

In the 1960s, the suburbs were thought to be the home of conformist colonies seeking statuses. This was later debunked by Herbert Gans, who showed that suburban culture is a direct product of the kinds of people who inhabit them. Suburban living has its own set of drawbacks. There is a lack of public transportation and employment opportunities. Jobs are constantly being added to suburbia, however, minimizing those drawbacks. As they grow, though, suburbs will face more and more of the problems of big cities as listed above and also pollution, congestion, traffic, and racial/ethnic tensions.

Middle-class families tend to move out of the cities and into the suburbs while maintaining employment inside the central city. These families also continue making use of city services. What they don't do is pay taxes to the city. This causes a strain on the city's budget, forcing them to cut services (police, fire, and medical), leaving the residents of the city negatively impacted.

Chapter Review

Activity 1: Multiple Choice

Identify the correct answer to the question.

1. Population growth is affected by which factors?
   A. Migration
   B. Birth rate
   C. Death rate
   D. All of the above

2. Gesellischaft includes:
   A. Emotionally committed relationships
   B. Impersonal relationships
   C. A strong sense of camaraderie or shared membership
   D. A community where most people know each other

3. The study of populations, including examining any changes over time, distribution, and composition, is called what?
   A. Urban planning
   B. Etiology
   C. Demography
   D. Ecology

4. Which theory hypothesizes that populations tend to grow exponentially which is much faster than the food supply does?
   A. Malthusian theory
   B. Demographic transition theory
   C. Human ecology
   D. Demographic explosion

5. Which of the following is not a push factor?
   A. Inadequate housing
   B. Good employment prospects
   C. Overpopulation
   D. Bad weather

6. Which of the following is not a pull factor?
   A. Freedoms
   B. Good employment prospects
   C. Inadequate housing
   D. Pleasant weather

Activity 2: Short Answer
Answer the questions or prompts as fully as possible using the knowledge you have gained in this chapter.

1. What is urbanization?

2. What is the difference between fertility and fecundity?

3. What are the stages of the demographic transition process and the key reason why each is titled as it is?

4. What is the difference between an immigrant and an emigrant?

Chapter Review Answers

Activity 1:
1. D
2. B
3. C
4. A
5. B
6. C

Activity 2:
1. Urbanization is the process of people moving from rural areas into cities.
2. Fertility involves the actual average of babies born every year per female of child-bearing age. Fecundity is an estimate of the maximum child-bearing potential of each.
3. 1: High birth & death rate: no birth control or medical aid 2: High birth & low death: medical aid improves
4. Immigrants are people who are moving into a country. Emigrants are those moving out of a country.

Chapter 7: Social Processes, Part 2

What's the point?

- To identify sources of social change.
- To know relevant theories of social change.
- To understand collective behavior.
- To differentiate the kinds of crowds.
- To accurately identify types of mass behavior.
- To identify social movements.

Societies change – sometimes slowly and inevitably, sometimes rapidly and with great effort. This chapter explores the social processes involved in that change, including mass behavior and social movement theory.

Social Change

Social change is a process of altering patterns of social behavior, social relationships, and social structures over time. For example, over the last 200 years, America has changes from an agricultural society to an industrial society. Over that same time span, other societies have not changed as much. Sociologists aim to explore the reasons for those differences and the dynamics of the actual changes. August Comte, the first to coin the term 'sociology,' thought that the study of social change could make it possible to plan the future.

Theories

Sociocultural-Evolution Theory:
Sociocultural evolution is the tendency for social structures to become more complex over time. This theory asserts that some simple societies grow from simple hunting-and-gathering societies into industrial and postindustrial societies. There are many patterns of development with variations available in each path; not every society forms the same, takes the same course, or grows at the same pace.

Functionalist Theory:
Talcott Parsons elaborated on Emile Durkheim's functionalist base to create a theory that explained social change. Parsons dictated that the different interdependent parts of society all contribute to that society's health and strength. He posited that a change in one aspect of a

society causes changes in other parts as the entire system seeks a new equilibrium. Thus, social change occurs out of the needs of every part.

Conflict Theory:
Conflict theorists focus on the conflict and tensions between all competing interests in a society, whether they are class or social tensions. They feel that conflict is inevitable and a normal part of change. Conflict theory does not adequately explain all forms of social change, but this theory is particularly adept at explaining such social change phenomena as civil rights and women's rights.

The World-System Model:
This theory explains social change as the handiwork of a group of core nations within the world system. The three types of countries that exist in this model include:

- Core countries: those with a powerful economy and military who are highly industrialized.
  - These countries manufacture products from raw materials that are supplied by peripheral countries.
- Peripheral countries: those with a weak economy and military who depend on the exportation of their raw materials to the core countries.
  - These countries are forced to follow the economic structure of the core countries which keeps peripheral countries poor and weak.
- Semiperiphery countries: those that are between peripheral and core because they are moving toward industrialization.

Sources

Cultural Influences:
A society's culture affects its processes. A subtle shift in culture can echo into the society as a whole and reverberate into social change. There are three cultural sources of social change:

- Discovery: A new perception of an aspect of an already-known reality. When this new knowledge is acted on, it can induce social change.
- Invention: A combination of existing and new knowledge to create something new. All inventions are dependent on past knowledge. Inventions can change society drastically.
- Cultural diffusion: the spread of cultural elements from one society to another through trade, travel, migration, conquest, etc. These newly imported elements can cause changes in thoughts and processes and lead to social change.

Population:

Significant increases and decreases in population (especially over a relatively short time period) will impact, and possibly even disrupt, a society's systems. On the other hand, a population that grows too slow could face extinction. In today's world, overpopulation is the greatest population threat. (See the previous chapter for a review of that term.) Social change occurs as the social structure and systems attempt to meet the needs of the increased or decreased population.

Technology:

As a major source of social change, technology is the practical application of knowledge (scientific or otherwise). Most technological innovations are derived from existing knowledge and technology. More advanced societies will produce technological change at a faster rate, and thus, social change will be at a faster rate. Technological determinism is the idea that available technology determines a society's culture, social structure, and history. This may be true in many societies, if not all. Once technology is used and society becomes used to its advantages, it is easily and quickly adopted.

Another aspect of technological influence is cultural lag, the delay that exists between a technological development and the cultivation of an adequate cultural understanding and interaction with it.

Economic Development and Modernization:

Modernization refers to the process of economic, cultural, and social change that must occur for a society to transform into an industrial society. Some sociologists claim that all societies are on their way to becoming an industrial or postindustrial society. There are three components of modernization:

1. Industrialization: A shift from human to non-human energy used during the manufacturing process.
2. Urbanization: Movement from rural to urban areas where manufacturing factories are located.
3. Bureaucratization: An increase in large, formal organizations.

Economic relationships also change during modernization. Some more changes that take place as a society modernizes include:

- Labor shifts from primary sector to secondary
- New occupations are created
- Mobility increases, both geographically and socially
- Achieved status replaces ascribed status
- Religion becomes less important
- Mass media and culture expands
- Centralized political power grows

As modernization occurs, <u>convergence theory</u> tends to come to fruition. This theory states that all societies are becoming more alike due to modernization. This theory is rather controversial, though, because of the sheer number of societies, the varied types and stages of development they are each in.

Revolution:
A <u>revolution</u> is a violent overthrow of an existing social system or political authority. This method of social change is dramatic and involves mass violence and radical societal restructuring. Over a short time period, a revolution challenges and, if successful, changes the existing social order. Societies that exhibit the following behaviors or attitudes are ripe for revolution:

- Widespread grievances
- Rising expectations
- Blockage of change
- Loss of legitimacy
- Breakdown of military

Collective Behavior

<u>Collective behavior</u> is the spontaneous action of people trying to work out common responses to ambiguous situations that are unpredictable, unstructured, and unstable. Collective behaviors include crowds, riots, fads, and public opinion.

Collective behavior is hard to study because it is unstructured. It can also be difficult to trace underlying causations and regularities from one incident to the next. Another reason it is difficult to study is its commonly spontaneous nature. Researchers have been able to identify five factors or conditions that can lead to a collective behavior episode:

- Environmental factors: Timing and ease of communication add to the likelihood of spontaneous behavior.
- Lack of norms: An absence of developed norms that will guide actions.
- Conflicting values and norms: The existence of contradictory cultural elements.
- Relative deprivation: The occurrence of people not having what they think they deserve.
- Breakdown of social control: A failure of police to perform their roles or a loss of confidence in the system.

Theories

Value-Added Theory:
Developed by Neil Smelser, this theory identifies six conditions that must be present for any

type of collective behavior to occur. This theory helps to identify the conditions that underlie collective behavior. His social conditions include:

- Structural conduciveness: A social structure that allows collective behavior to occur.
- Structural strain: The perception that something is wrong.
- Generalized belief: An analysis of what is wrong, how things should be, and how the problem is corrected.
- Precipitating factors: The spark that lights the fire; the often dramatic event that stimulates action.
- Mobilization of participants: Action! Vague norms emerge.
- Social control: shapes or constrains the other five requirements.

Contagion Theory:
The French sociologist Gustave Le Bon developed this theory to explain crowd behavior as the result of infectious emotion and action. Individuality is lost in the collective mind of the crowd. This collective mind is caused by:

- Invincibility: Apparent power in numbers
- Contagion: Rapid infection of ideas
- Suggestibility: The likelihood of agreeing with ideas

Emergent-Norms Theory:
Lewis Killian explained crowd behavior as a result of norms that arise in the process of social interaction. In this theory, conformity to the groups explains the behavior of the crowd. The norms of the group explain what behaviors are accepted in crowd situations and are initiated from the visible actions of a few. Even those who disagree with the norms remain silent and passive; in other words they support it by not voicing or acting against it.

Crowds
Crowds are temporary groups of people who are in close proximity to one another and who have a common focus. In general, crowds are unstable and have little structure and few, if any, elaborate goals or plans. Crowds operate with a sense of urgency and are unable to support themselves for long. Most collective behaviors occur in crowds. The different types of crowds include:

- Casual crowd: A loosely structured, usually passive group with little emotional interaction. Members enter and leave at will.
  - Example: Bystanders who witness an altercation on the street.
- Conventional crowd: More structured with more predictable behavior. Members choose to be a part.
  - Example: Concert-goers
- Expressive crowd: Structured around a celebration or event and allows expressive

emotions.
  o Example: Concert-goers, sporting event attendees
- Solidaristic crowds: Members have a strong sense of unity or agreement.
  o Example: Political party rally
- Acting crowds: An expressive crowd turned angry and hostile.
  o Two types of acting crowds:
    - Mobs: Threatens violence or is violent toward a single target. Mobs usually have a leader and at least a minimum amount of structure.
    - Riots: Violent and angry toward multiple, changing, targets and includes looting, property damage, and assault. Riots usually include members of groups who have been discriminated against.

Mass Behavior

While crowds are physically close and able to affect each other directly, mass behavior is a widely dispersed crowd that does not have face-to-face contact but who still influences one another indirectly through common sources of information. Mass behavior doesn't have to be negative or unpleasant. There are several types:

- Fashion: A temporarily popular style of dress or behavior that departs from what is customary. Fashion is often seen as a status symbol.
- Fad: A temporary fascination followed by a large number of people. Fads can be either object, idea, activity, or personality-based.
- Craze: An intense fad that leaves lasting consequences and becomes part of the culture when it ends.
- Panic: A collective behavior of those facing an incoming threat; fear, spontaneity, and lack of coordination are hallmarks of panic actions. Cooperative social relationships break down causing more fear and danger.
- Mass hysteria: a widespread anxiety that is caused by an irrational belief and results in irrational behavior. This hysteria can be contained in one community, or it can involve a larger part of society. When the perceived threat is proven non-existent, the hysteria subsides.
- Disaster behavior: following natural disasters, normal activities are disrupted and heterogeneous groups develop in the face of the chaotic aftermath. Disaster behavior is usually positive and acts as an aid. Prolonged exposure to disaster, however, can leave a lasting negative effect on a community.

Communication is a necessary part of mass behavior. Some forms of communication can be viewed as basic types of collective behaviors in their own rights. Some of the types of mass communication are:

- Rumor: An unconfirmed piece of information passed from one person to another (and another and so on). When people are uninformed or suspect the information of being suspect, rumors are more likely to be generated. Rumors are usually not true and are far easier to start than to stop.

- Gossip: Non-essential discussion of another's personal lives and actions.
- Mass media: The strongest force shaping public opinion, these forms of media (newspaper, television, internet, and radio) aim to reach as much of the population as possible.
- Urban legends: Realistic but untrue stories that often have a twist or irony concerning a recent event(s). These are collective responses to uncertain situations and usually provide a lesson or warning.

Social Movements

Another form of collective behavior is a <u>social movement</u>, a large group of people joined together to bring about or resist a social or cultural change. Examples include the women's rights movement and the environmental movement. These organized and goal-directed efforts are usually enduring and have been the source of major social change. While collective behavior is more unstructured and spontaneous, social movements are deliberate and organized; they are more likely to occur in industrial countries rather than preindustrial. The most common types of social movement include:

- Reform movements: Seek to improve society; they are the most common and are generally accepted by society.
- Revolutionary movements: Seek to overthrow or replace an existing social structure; they develop when participants are dissatisfied with the government's inattention or rejection.
  - Few revolutionary movements have been successful; those that have been have brought great change and influenced societies across the globe.
- Resistance (regressive) movements: Seek to reverse or resist change and revert society to more traditional values.
- Expressive (utopian) movements: seek to create "perfect societies" by separating from the larger society and establishing a community that promises to meet every need.
- Millenarian (religious) movements: seek to disrupt religious or spiritual practices.

Social movements bring many problems into the consciousness of the society that many would ignore otherwise. During the life of the social movement, four stages represent the progress that leads to societal acceptance.

Stage	Description of Stage
Preliminary	Social restlessness; conflict between groups. Members strive to support their views. Leaders emerge
Popular	Discontented unite with others who share views. Objectives are supported; movement becomes respectable. Leaders emerge as prophets or reformers.
Formal organization	Values and goals become clear; organizational structure develops. Movement becomes centered on administrative tasks.
Institutional	Movement becomes accepted as part of society. Idealism and fervor is dulled and lost.

Figure 10: Life Course of Social Movements

Another type of social movement that is especially dreaded is <u>terrorism</u>, the violent use of force against civilians to intimidate a society. Authoritarian and totalitarian governments use terror against their own populations as a means of control.

Theories

Relative Deprivation Theory:
This theory asserts that social movements occur when people in the society feel deprived when compared either to others or the society's past lifestyle. Social movements are more common in affluent societies than in those that experience poverty.

Resource Mobilization Theory:
This theory asserts that social movements are dependent on the ability of its members to organize and use resources (time, money, people, and skills). This theory explains how movements are started and successful.

Chapter Review

Activity 1: Multiple Choice

Identify the correct answer to the question.

1. This theory explains how individuality is seemingly erased by the influential spread of group action and emotion.
    A. Mass hysteria
    B. Conventional theory
    C. Contagion theory
    D. Emergent-norms theory

2. What characteristic describes a member of an expressive crowd?
    A. Does not follow well-established norms
    B. Is seeking an emotional outlet
    C. Is looking for personal gratification
    D. Desires to do harm to society

3. The process of altering patterns of social behavior, social relationships, and social structures over time is called what?
    A. Collective change
    B. Social movement
    C. Social micromanagement
    D. Social change

4. The delay that exists between a technological development and the cultivation of an adequate cultural understanding and interaction with it is called what?
    A. Social change
    B. Social diffusion
    C. Cultural lag
    D. Cultural borrowing

5. Groups of people that desire to promote or resist change in society through organized means are called what?
    A. Social movements
    B. Mass behavior
    C. Cultural change
    D. Collective behavior

6. Which theory asserts that societies become more like each other as they evolve?
   A. Conventional theory
   B. Convergence theory
   C. Emergent-norms theory
   D. Traditional theory

7. The process of a society evolving into an industrial society is known as:
   A. Cultural lag
   B. Terrorism
   C. Revolution
   D. Modernization

8. _____ is the idea that available technology determines a society's culture, social structure, and history.
   A. Revolution
   B. Social movement
   C. Technological determinism
   D. Cultural lag

9. The combination of existing and new knowledge to create something new is which one of the sources of social change listed below:
   A. Discovery
   B. Invention
   C. Cultural diffusion
   D. None of the above

10. Moving from rural areas into urban areas is called:
    A. Urbanization
    B. Modernization
    C. Revolution
    D. Terrorism

Activity 2: Short Answer

Answer the questions or prompts as fully as possible using the knowledge you have gained in this chapter.

1. Define collective behavior.

2. What conditions make collective behavior more likely to occur?

3. List and describe the different types of crowds.

4. What is the primary distinction between crowds and mass behavior?

5. Explain the difference between mobs and riots.

6. List the four types of mass communication described in the text.

7. List the types of mass behavior discussed in the text.

8. List the types of social movements.

Chapter Review Answers

Activity 1:

1. C
2. B
3. D
4. C
5. A
6. B
7. D
8. C
9. B
10. A

Activity 2:
1. Collective behavior is the spontaneous actions of people attempting to work out common responses to ambiguous situations that are unpredictable, unstructured, and unstable.
2. When environmental factors, a lack of norms, conflicting values or norms, relative deprivation, and a breakdown of social control exist, collective behavior is almost certain.
3. Casual – loosely structured with nothing to link members. Conventional – members choose to be a part of this more structured behavior. Expressive – centered around a specific event; emotional. Solidaristic – members are united and/or in agreement. Acting crowds – expressive crowds that have turned angry or hostile (mobs & riots).
4. Crowds are groups that are in close proximity to one another. Mass behavior are those widely dispersed.
5. Mobs are violent toward a specific target while riots are violent toward multiple, sporadically changing, targets.
6. Mass communication types include: rumor, gossip, mass media, and urban legends.
7. Mass behaviors include: fashion, fad, craze, panic, mass hysteria, and disaster behavior.
8. Social movements include: reform movements, revolutionary movements, resistance (regressive) movements, expressive (utopian) movements, millenarian (religious) movements.

Practice Exam

Directions: Each of the questions or incomplete statements below is followed by five suggested answers or completions. Select the one that is best in each case.

1. Who created the three categories of suicide (egoistic, altruistic, and anomic)?
   A) August Comte
   B) Max Parsons
   C) Karl Marx
   D) Emile Durkheim

2. What is the term used to describe the belief that one should judge other cultures within the context of that culture, not by comparing it to one's own culture?
   A) Cultural relativism
   B) Contextual culture
   C) Egocentrism
   D) Sociology

3. What is the term to describe rules that govern behavior?
   A) Manners
   B) Social policies
   C) Norms
   D) None of the above

4. Which of the following is the variable that is used to indicate cause?
   A) Intervening
   B) Independent
   C) Catalyst
   D) Dependent

5. Strongly held beliefs within a culture based on moral convictions are called:
   A) Assumptions
   B) Mores
   C) Norms
   D) Constructs

6. Margolyn, an astronaut, finds time in her busy schedule to play dodgeball with a team and attend weekly trivia. Her dodgeball and trivia activities make up her _____.
   A) Master statuses
   B) Prescribed statuses
   C) Subordinate statuses
   D) Recreational statuses

7. What sociological theory focuses on homeostasis, the integration of its parts, and the stability of social systems?
   A) Functionalist
   B) Social balance theory
   C) Symbolic interactionist
   D) Functionalist

8. What is the term used to describe when a person makes a judgment about other societies based upon the values and beliefs of their own society?
   A) Ethnocentrism
   B) Egocentrism
   C) Prejudice
   D) Cultural shock

9. Who originally coined the word "sociology"?
   A) Karl Marx
   B) Auguste Comte
   C) Emile Durkheim
   D) None of the above

10. Researchers decide to test the correlation between the effects of a film on race relations with students' level of prejudice. In this case, what kind of variable is prejudice?
    A) Independent
    B) Dependent
    C) Effect
    D) Causal

11. What is the name of the sociological theory that uses the analogy of individuals as actors who may portray many different roles?
    A) Multiple roles
    B) Dramaturgical
    C) Functionalist
    D) Social relativism

12. What would be an informal sanction of shoplifting?
    A) Your date cancelling because they don't want to be associated with a thief
    B) A week-long imprisonment
    C) Having to do 20 hours of community service
    D) All of the above

13. _____ are patterns of social life that appear in all societies.
    A) Cultural universals
    B) Norms
    C) Global socialism
    D) Folkways

14. Which of the following is an example of ethnocentrism?
    A) Mary meets a graduate student from China and finds her cultural traditions fascinating
    B) David travels to another country and thinks that their practice of worshipping many gods is primitive and ignorant
    C) Shelly visits friends in Japan and finds eating raw seafood unappealing
    D) Michelle visits a foreign country and finds it difficult to learn the language and to adjust to the diet

15. All of the following characteristics are true regarding Max Weber's model of bureaucracy, EXCEPT:
    A) Power is distributed hierarchically
    B) There is a fixed set of rules and regulations
    C) Rules are to be meted out impartially
    D) All of the above are characteristics of bureaucracies

16. What is the most important difference between folkways and mores, according to sociologists?
    A) Mores are found only among a certain class
    B) A violation of folkway leads to severe punishment
    C) Violations of folkways are not considered crimes
    D) Folkways include customary behavior

17. All of the following statements about primary groups are true, EXCEPT:
    A) They engage in intimate communication
    B) They last for a very long time
    C) They possess a limited knowledge of other group members
    D) All of the above are true

18. Dr. Findlay is an expert on African religions. She finds the widespread religious practice of performing clitoridectomies on young girls to be disturbing, but believes it can be studied and understood, given the social norms and values of the society. Dr. Findlay is adopting what kind of attitude?
    A) Ethnocentrism
    B) Cultural relativism
    C) Multiculturalism
    D) None of the above

19. In order to learn about a particular social phenomenon, Max Weber believed he needed to understand the point of view of the subject. The term used to describe this method is _____.
    A) Verstehen
    B) Social statics
    C) Counter-ethnocentrism
    D) Symbolic interaction

20. Who formulated the first formal "structural strain of theory" of sociology?
    A) Karl Marx
    B) Edwin Sutherland
    C) Robert Merton
    D) Walter Reckless

21. Which of the following group of characteristics best illustrates the notion of ascribed statuses?
    A) Male, African-American, Age 45
    B) Female, Married, Pregnant
    C) Female, Age 25, Oncologist
    D) Male, Jewish, Rabbi

22. The Strain n Theory best explains _____.
    A) Marijuana cultivation
    B) Speeding
    C) Social Norms
    D) Robbery

23. Rigid endogamy is associated with which type of system?
    A) Polygamy
    B) Caste
    C) Class
    D) All of the above

24. Jenny is a worker in your place of employment. For the past eight months, you've been going out with Jenny socially. Jenny would be considered a part of your _____.
    A) Primary group
    B) Social circle
    C) Secondary group
    D) Social group

25. Several people are waiting for the bus at the bus stop. They don't interact with each other, and they have no sense of belonging together. This is called a(n) _____.
    A) Stratified group
    B) Aggregate
    C) Primary group
    D) Secondary group

26. Which of the following best defines anomie?
    A) A society where no laws exist
    B) When people don't know the social rules or when they lose faith in them
    C) Something that is out of the ordinary
    D) None of the above

27. Sociologists use the term 'deviant behavior' to describe behaviors which a certain group defines as _____.
    A) The general standards to follow
    B) Too risky to engage in
    C) Violating basic norms
    D) All of the above

28. Steve's mother was a cashier at a local convenience store, and Steve is a professor of biology at a prestigious university. What is this an example of?
    A) Structural mobility
    B) Cross-generational mobility
    C) Imbalance mobility
    D) Intergenerational mobility

29. According to Sutherland's theory of differential association, deviance is attributed to _____.
    A) Attachments to others who are also deviant
    B) Poor parenting in early childhood
    C) Biological differences between deviants and non-deviants
    D) Lack of structure in multiple life areas

30. The idea that all Irish Americans are alcoholics, or that all African-Americans are lazy is an example of:
   A) Stereotypes
   B) Prejudice
   C) Targeting
   D) Discrimination

31. Robert Bales discovered that most groups have two types of leaders, _____ and _____.
   A) Authoritarian and authoritative
   B) Instrumental and expressive
   C) Rigid and flexible
   D) Friendly and goal-oriented

32. Wendy has been tardy for class for several weeks in a row and her lateness has become disruptive to her classmates. As a result, her classmates scorn her. The behavior of Wendy's classmates is an example of a(n):
   A) Group-defined norm
   B) Bullying
   C) Formal sanction
   D) Informal sanction

33. Which of the following would be considered a defining characteristic of a closed stratification system?
   A) Heredity plays a large part in determining one's status within the stratification system
   B) The boundaries between classes are poorly defined and people can cross them unnoticed
   C) There are rigid boundaries between classes that are difficult or impossible for people to cross
   D) Immigration from other countries is forbidden

34. Which of the following examples are forms of institutional discrimination?
   I.   A geographic mismatch between workers and jobs following the move of a company from inner-city
   II.   A landlord's distaste for Latino tenants causes him to reject all applicants with Hispanic surnames
   III.   During an economic downturn, a policy of "last hired is the first fired" has resulted in a disproportionate layoff of women and minorities
   IV.   The administration of IQ and other standardized tests
      A) I only
      B) I and II only
      C) II and III only
      D) I, III, and IV

35. Who are sociologists referring to when they use the term 'ethnic group'?
    A) People who share the same viewpoints on politics
    B) People who have a shared cultural heritage
    C) People who have the same occupation
    D) People who share the same food tastes

36. Which of the following best describes social mobility?
    A) The downward movement of individuals in a society
    B) The upward and downward movement of groups or individuals within a stratification system
    C) The upward movement of groups in a society
    D) None of the above

37. Stratification on the basis of race:
    I.   Is based on biological differences in groups of people which are translated, genetically, into different behavioral and personality traits
    II.   Is synonymous with slavery since historically people have been enslaved on the basis of skin color
    III. Has often been justified by an ideology (racism) which contends that some races are innately superior to others
    IV.   Is insignificant compared to other stratification systems such as those   based on age or gender
        A) I only
        B) II only
        C) III only
        D) I, II, and IV only

38. Which of the following describes a group of people who share certain physical and/or cultural characteristics, and who are victims of prejudice and discrimination?
    A) Minority group
    B) Primary group
    C) Marginalized group
    D) Ethnic group

39. The Supreme Court case of Brown v. Board of Education (1954) declared what activity to be unconstitutional?
    A) Gender discrimination
    B) School segregation
    C) Housing discrimination
    D) Corporal punishment

40. According to Marx, who are the owners of the means of production?
    A) Capitalists
    B) Upper class
    C) Elitists
    D) Bourgeois

41. Many school systems place students in classes based on their ability, social class, or other characteristics. What is this an example of?
    A) Talented placement
    B) Latent functions of education
    C) Tracking
    D) None of the above

42. Which of the following statements is true about intragenerational mobility?
    A) It is a product of one's upbringing
    B) It is a change in social position within one's lifetime
    C) It is the same thing as cross-generational mobility
    D) It always results in downward mobility

43. _____ is the formalized enactment of religious beliefs.
    A) Rituals
    B) Dogma
    C) Enlightenment
    D) Praying

44. Which of the following is an example of upward social mobility?
    A) The daughter of a banker becomes a musician
    B) A professor's son working as a park ranger
    C) A rancher's son becomes President of the United States
    D) All of the above

45. According to the functionalist theory, all of the following are functions of educational institutions EXCEPT:
    A) Providing childcare
    B) Creating future citizens
    C) Preparing young people for social change
    D) Teaching life skills

46. In what kind of society is there a norm which permits a man to have more than one wife at a time?
    A) Serial monogamy
    B) Polyandry
    C) Polygyny
    D) None of the above

47. Which of the following does the sociology of religion focus on?
    A) The social characteristics and consequences of religion
    B) How close one's group can get to God
    C) The afterlife
    D) All of the above

48. Regarding marriage, the majority of couples share which of the following characteristics?
    I. Social class background
    II. Educational level
    III. Racial background
    IV. Personality traits
    A) I only
    B) I and II only
    C) III and IV only
    D) I, II, and III only

49. What are conflict theorists pointing to when they refer to a 'hidden curriculum'?
    A) The school budget that is not made public knowledge
    B) The passing on of values and norms in school that perpetuate the existing system of stratification
    C) The parts of the curriculum that parents are not made aware of
    D) The courses that only certain students are allowed to enroll in

50. What is religion, according to Karl Marx?
    A) It allows groups to express their spiritual convictions
    B) It reaffirms the social bonds people have with each other
    C) It is an ideology that supports the ideas of the ruling class
    D) All of the above

51. What does polytheism refer to?
    A) The worship of more than one god
    B) The worship of animal spirits
    C) The worship of a single god
    D) The blending of several religions

52. The power elite model originated in the work of:
    A) C. Wright Mills
    B) Karl Marx
    C) Emile Durkheim
    D) Mark Weber

53. Which of the following theorists argued that religion should be viewed as the "opiate of the masses"?
    A) Emile Durkheim
    B) Karl Marx
    C) Max Weber
    D) Sigmund Freud

54. Who would ask the question: "What causes the disease?"
    A) Medical doctors
    B) Functionalists
    C) Sociologists
    D) Epidemiologists

55. Which best describes the process of secularization?
    A) People are always influenced by religious beliefs
    B) People seek new religious interpretations
    C) People are less influenced by religious beliefs
    D) People who return to traditional religious beliefs

56. What is religion, according to Karl Marx?
    I. An institution of the elite
    II. The center of all conflict
    III. Appealing to the masses because it provides an escape from reality
    A) I only
    B) II only
    C) III only
    D) I and III only

57. What is the name of the system by which goods and services are produced, distributed, and consumed?
    A) The economic system
    B) The global economy
    C) The industrial system
    D) The barter system

58. How is marriage viewed in most pre-industrial societies, marriage is viewed as:
    I. A formal arrangement between individuals who are bonded by romantic love
    II. A polygynous arrangement between three individuals
    III. A formal arrangement between two individuals who share similar social characteristics
    IV. A practical economic arrangement
    A) I only
    B) II and IV only
    C) I and IV only
    D) IV only

59. "Policy should improve access to health care for minority racial and ethnic groups, the poor and women." This statement reflects _____.
    A) Conflict theory
    B) Functionalism
    C) Social justice
    D) Epidemiological

60. Susie has decided to take a couple of pain relievers because she has a headache. After taking the pills, Susie heads off to work for her five-hour shift. In sociological terms, Susie's headache is an example of a(n) _____.
    A) Sickness
    B) Illness
    C) Hindrance
    D) Medical condition

61. Years ago, alcoholics were considered to be moral failures, drunks, and deviants. Today, alcoholism is viewed and treated as a disease. This is an example of _____.
    A) An acute disease
    B) An illness
    C) Medicalization
    D) Societal shifts

62. Which of the following statements would be most consistent with the approach of conflict theory to the explanation of social stratification and social inequality?
    A) Social stratification persists because it is a rational system for distributing resources
    B) Social inequality persists because it works to motivate people to make a contribution to society.
    C) Social inequality exists because the poor cannot find stable employment/means of income
    D) Social inequality persists because the well-to-do use their monopoly over resources to dominate and exploit those with fewer resources

63. All of the following groups are included in C. Wright Mills' concept of the "power elite", EXCEPT for the _____.
    A) Political elite
    B) Media elite
    C) Economic elite
    D) None of the above

64. What is then notion of the "sick role" is associated with?
    A) Conflict theory
    B) Epidemiology
    C) Functionalism
    D) All of the above

65. According to Max Weber, what is the authority derived from the understanding that individuals have clearly defined rights and duties to uphold and that they implement rules and procedures impersonally?
    A) Legal-rational authority
    B) Legitimate authority
    C) Expert authority
    D) Charismatic authority

66. Which of the following describes a feeling of powerlessness and separation from society?
    A) Alienation
    B) Ostracization
    C) Passivity
    D) Depression

67. Who published the essay "Urbanism as a Way of Life"?
    A) Karl Marx
    B) Louis Wirth
    C) Ernest Burgess
    D) Emile Durkheim

68. What is the term used to describe the biological potential to give birth?
    A) Fecundity
    B) Genetics
    C) Fertility
    D) Population growth potential

69. The following statement is an example of what: "Birth rates are lower in nations with high levels of economic development."
    A) A positive correlation
    B) Reverse correlation
    C) Negative correlation
    D) Circular correlation

70. Dylan, who lives in Kentucky, gets a job offer in California where the pay is excellent, living conditions are good, and there are more single women. Dylan's decision to migrate is based upon which of the following factors?
    A) Push factors
    B) Pull factors
    C) Demographics
    D) All of the above

71. Which of the following best describes people who first moved to the suburbs?
    A) Wealthy
    B) Blue-collar workers
    C) Agricultural workers
    D) All of the above

72. Tonnies argued that communities where relationships are personal and intimate may be called _____.
    A) Secondary groups
    B) Socially constructed
    C) Gesellschaft
    D) Gemeinschaft

73. Since World War II, this group has had the greatest increase in labor force participation rate.
    A) Women
    B) Teenagers
    C) Men
    D) Latino-Americans

74. According to the theory of the demographic transition, what does the final stage in the transition process results in?
    A) Low birth rates and high death rates
    B) High birth rates and low death rates
    C) Low birth rates and low death rates
    D) None of the above

75. All of the following are push factors in migration, EXCEPT _____.
    A) Lack of employment opportunities
    B) Political oppression
    C) Travel costs
    D) Poor climatic conditions

76. The net increase and decrease of a population depends on which of the following factors?
    I. Migration
    II. Fertility
    III. Mortality
    IV. Urbanization
    A) I only
    B) I, II, and III only
    C) I and II only
    D) I and IV only

77. Fans at a rock concert respond to the music and mood by raucous shouting and screaming, dancing with one another in the aisle and in front of the stage, and throwing flowers onto the stage. These fans would be characterized as what kind of crowd?
    A) An expressive crowd
    B) An acting crowd
    C) A rioting mob
    D) Diehard fans

78. People are more likely to do what in gellschaft compared to people in geminschaft?
    A) Be tradition-oriented
    B) Seek unity by sharing a goal
    C) Seek advice from close contacts
    D) See others as a means of advancing their own individual goals

79. Fecundity can be explained as:
    A) The possibility of having a female who can carry on the reproductive genes
    B) The ratio of males to females in any given group
    C) The number of times a woman can get married and reproduce
    D) The potential number of children a woman can have during her childbearing years

80. Studies show that as one's education level increases, prejudice decreases. This illustrates what kind of relationship between education and prejudice?
    A) Definitive
    B) Causal
    C) Negative correlation
    D) Positive correlation

81. What is the name for groups that act with some continuity and organization to promote or resist changes in society?
    A) Collective behavior
    B) Cultural change
    C) Social movements
    D) Societal movements

82. Which sociological theory contains concepts such as exploitation, inequality, and power relationships?
    A) Conflict
    B) Functionalist
    C) Dramaturgical
    D) Evolutionary

83. According to Shelby, the norms and values of her culture are more rational and advanced than the norms and values of other cultures she has come into contact with. Which of the following best describes Shelby's current belief system?
    A) She is stereotyping another culture
    B) She is being ethnocentric
    C) She is being egocentric
    D) She is expressing prejudices

84. Which of the following statements about collective behavior is incorrect?
    A) Collective situations usually have unclear goals and expectations
    B) Collective behavior is patterned behavior
    C) Collective behavior always represents the actions of groups of people
    D) Collective behavior is an ordinary part of people's everyday life

85. _____ is the primary subject of sociology.
    A) The individual
    B) Traditions and customs
    C) The group
    D) The school system

86. Sociologists use the term 'voluntary association' to refer to an organization which _____.
    A) Engages in retail sales
    B) Selects new members on the basis of merit
    C) Members join to pursue common interests
    D) Discriminates against those who do not voluntarily join the group

87. What is the name for the research method that follows a group of subjects over a period of time?
    A) Longitudinal study
    B) Cross-sectional study
    C) Survey
    D) Cross-generational study

88. While _____ are established standards to behavior, _____ legitimize them.
    A) Roles; values
    B) Mores; cultures
    C) Values; behaviors
    D) Norms; values

89. A professor who presents herself to her students as competent and knowledgeable is probably involved in what, according to Goffman?
    A) Status inconsistency
    B) Impression management activities
    C) Status performance
    D) All of the above

90. Max Weber was the first to discuss the essential characteristics of bureaucracy. One of these is _____.
    A) Equal authority among members of the organization
    B) Workers develop skills at a variety of tasks/trades
    C) Decisions are made in a democratic fashion
    D) A clearly defined chain of command

91. Sammie, a tenured professor at an elite college, accepts an offer to teach at another elite college in a neighboring city. Her move is an example of _____.
    A) Status mobility
    B) Horizontal mobility
    C) Vertical mobility
    D) None of the above

92. Which of the following theories of deviant behavior is based on the symbolic interactionist perspective?
    A) Sutherland's differential association theory
    B) Merton's anomie theory
    C) Sheldon's body type theory
    D) Lombroso's theory of atavism

93. A lawyer whose client is convicted of selling marijuana argues against sending the first-time offender to prison because of the likelihood of his learning more about crime. Which theory of deviance best supports his argument?
    A) Control theory
    B) Deviance theory
    C) Cultural transmission theory
    D) Deviance transmission theory

94. The division of society into status positions is called:
    A) The power elite
    B) Social segregation
    C) Stratification
    D) Demographical differentiation

95. All of the following statements about formal organizations are true, EXCEPT _____.
    A) A complex division of labor
    B) A hierarchy of ranked positions
    C) Continuity beyond organizational membership
    D) They are comprised of small, intimate groups

96. What is the term used for groups that have broken off from an established church?
    A) Sub-religions
    B) Cults
    C) Sects
    D) Secular churches

97. What is the name for the inequality and discrimination that result from the regular workings of a society?
    A) Segregation
    B) Prejudice
    C) Racism
    D) Institutional racism

98. Max Weber is best known for his study, _____.
    A) The Protestant Ethic and the Spirit of Capitalism
    B) Street Corner Society
    C) The Human Group
    D) The Division of Labor in Society

99. While _____ is an action or behavior directed at a particular group,_____refers to the attitude or belief held about this group.
    A) Discrimination; ageism
    B) Ethnocentrism; racism
    C) Discrimination; prejudice
    D) Scapegoating; prejudice

100. The sociologist's interest in race is due to the fact that:
     I. Race, as a biological fact, helps to determine and explain people's behavior
     II. Stratification on the basis of race predates all other forms of stratification
     III. People attach meaning and values to real or imagined group differences
     IV. Race is the basis for discrimination against all minority groups
        A) II only
        B) III only
        C) I and IV only
        D) None of the above

Practice Exam Answer Key

1. D	35. B	69. C
2. A	36. B	70. B
3. C	37. C	71. A
4. B	38. A	72. D
5. B	39. B	73. A
6. C	40. D	74. C
7. D	41. C	75. C
8. A	42. B	76. B
9. B	43. A	77. A
10. B	44. C	78. D
11. C	45. C	79. D
12. A	46. C	80. C
13. A	47. A	81. C
14. B	48. D	82. A
15. D	49. B	83. B
16. D	50. C	84. D
17. C	51. A	85. C
18. B	52. A	86. C
19. A	53. B	87. A
20. C	54. D	88. D
21. A	55. C	89. B
22. D	56. C	90. D
23. B	57. A	91. B
24. A	58. D	92. A
25. B	59. A	93. C
26. B	60. B	94. C
27. C	61. C	95. D
28. D	62. D	96. C
29. A	63. B	97. D
30. A	64. C	98. A
31. B	65. A	99. C
32. D	66. A	100. B
33. C	67. B	
34. D	68. A	

Appendix

CPSIA information can be obtained
at www.ICGtesting.com
Printed in the USA
LVHW060857011122
732062LV00013B/988